THREE-WHEELERS

The complete history of trikes 1885-1995

CHRIS REES

THREE-WHEELERS

The complete history of trikes 1885-1995

First published 1995
Second edition published November 1997
© Bluestream Books 1997

Published by **Bluestream Books,**
1 Howard Road, Reigate, Surrey RH2 7JE
Tel: 01737 222030

Edited by Peter Filby
Page design by Jane Burdge
Typeset by Crocodile, Crawley
Repro by Digiscan, London
Printed by Grapevine Print & Marketing

Contents

Acknowledgements

Triple thankyous to everyone who has helped with this book. Special thanks to Gary Axon, Chris Booth, Phil Boothroyd, Stephen Boyd, Stan Cornock, Jean and Edwin Hammond, Rowan Isaac, Tom Lucas, Richard Martin, Charles Morgan and the Morgan Motor Company, Paul Negyesi, Henry Pollard, Mike Redwick-Jones, John Rose, Mike Shepherd, Derek Smith.

Even more thanks to Ian Hyne, whose passion for three-wheelers in *Kitcars International* magazine has helped so much to make this book a reality. As you'll see from the photograph on the foreword page, Ian is even barmy enough to go trialling every year in a Triking. The only surprise is that he doesn't yet own a three-wheeler.

It was Peter Filby's ownership of a Lomax that had much to do with generating his enthusiasm for trikes and giving him the courage to do something so reckless as publishing this book. Indeed, he became so enthusiastic that he insisted on writing several extra sections for the book. Thanks, Peter. And finally, thanks to Peter's own magazine, *Which Kit?*, for supplying so many photographs.

Foreword
by Ian Hyne

The first machine I ever drove for a magazine article was deficient to the tune of one wheel. Despite this apparent mechanical failing, I revelled in the novel experience of an 850cc engine providing a power-to-weight ratio of 200bhp per ton. Not only that, but the car's supreme standards of design and engineering allowed it to embarrass far more sophisticated and powerful four-wheelers around corners.

That machine was the Triking. Although not the easiest car to drive, eventual mastery of the linear gear change, lack of reverse and novel cornering techniques brought a surge of excitement. On that first date, I quickly learned that its abilities also extended off the road at hillclimb events. Just as exhilarating as piloting a Triking was providing the ballast on many a high speed ultra-steep ascent of a classic climb. Ever since that Triking drive, I have had the softest of spots for these unusual and deceptively capable machines. Somewhat harder to explain is why.

Part of the reason must be a touch of nostalgia for the greatest three-wheeler of all. No review of three-wheelers can ignore the Morgan, which has provided the inspiration for not only the Triking but dozens of other latter-day three-wheelers. In 1909 Henry Frederick Stanley Morgan crashed his 7HP Peugeot motorcycle and, while recovering, created his first three-wheeled car. The result was a classic example of the 'simplify and reduce weight' school of thought. Perhaps a little bit too simple: you got tiller steering, virtually no bodywork and exhaust pipes which acted as lower chassis tubes!

However primitive it was, it rapidly displayed its capacity to generate enormous driver enjoyment. With further development, that enjoyment was only matched by the exotic sports cars of the day. Had it not been for the Morgan's outstanding competition success on the track, on the road and on hillclimbs, three-wheelers might have died out completely. But they didn't. Thanks to HFS Morgan's legacy, the current crop of three-wheelers expresses everything which is best about the genre.

The very first steam and petrol cars were three-wheelers and they have had a consistent presence throughout motoring history. This fact – and a thousand others – is highlighted in this timely review of cars 'with one wheel missing', written by Chris Rees (himself the owner of a Bond Bug, Lomax and three-wheeled Citroen 2CV) and published by Peter Filby, another Lomax owner.

There are many reasons advanced for the superiority of three-wheelers over their four-wheeled counterparts but, in truth, having three wheels creates its own problems, problems which can be simply overcome by the addition of a fourth circular limb. For my part, I believe their popularity is entirely due to the fun they provide. Whether it's a 2CV based Lomax, a Moto Guzzi based Triking or a BMW powered Grinnall Scorpion, they all have one thing in common: they surprise the hell out of Sierra drivers!

Ian Hyne, Editor, Kitcars International

Bubbling over. Shot of a Heinkel from a late 1950s St. Trinian's film. Driver is George 'Arthur Daley' Cole.

Even world champion racing drivers are partial to three-wheel motoring. Recognise that face in the cockpit of the wild, BMW K75 powered Modulo? It's none other than Nigel Mansell.

Introduction

Three-wheelers. A national joke... somehow not quite 'proper' cars, not quite 'proper' motorbikes... dangerous... eccentric... laughable. This is the popular (mis)conception of a public brought up on a diet of Reliant Robins. To judge three-wheelers by such a narrow field of example is like judging all Englishmen by their football team's supporters abroad, or all XR3 drivers by the nerd who jumps you at a traffic light.

Ten years ago, you could not have written a book about three-wheelers. You would have been laughed away by a public almost completely uninterested in trikes. A lot has changed since then.

Since people rediscovered the fact that three-wheelers actually carry advantages over their more 'normal' four-wheeler brethren, there has been something of a three-wheeler renaissance. Not since the days of the bubble car have there been so many three-wheelers on offer as there are today.

The current, healthy crop of trikes is part of a group of what I would call true trikes. In other words, not four-wheelers missing one wheel, but trikes *designed* from the ground-up as three-wheelers, following correct engineering principles. Not Reliant Robins, but modern equivalents of the pre-war Morgans.

Alongside this growth in manufacturers, there has been a corresponding growth in the number of people who drive three-wheelers. They realise that they are typically fun-to-drive, lightweight, handsome machines: real sports cars, in fact. It is this group of people which has reinvented the three-wheeler. It's no longer an object of derision, but increasingly a distinct and respected branch of the motoring tree.

So why three wheels? There are appropriately three explanations: economy, legality and weight.

Economy is the reason why many of the earliest cars were three-wheelers. It was simply cheaper to make a vehicle with three wheels than four. But for reasons of stability, the four-wheelers became the norm and three-wheelers were marginalised as the absolute economy alternatives to 'real' motor cars. That raison d'etre remained in place at least until the 1960s, when increasing affluence at all levels put paid to the last of the austerity three-wheelers, the bubble cars.

Point number two: legality. The law is the only reason why Reliant still sells any Robins. In Britain (as indeed in many other countries), three-wheelers have a special legal status. As long as they weigh less than 8cwt (or, in these

How times have changed! Top photograph shows a 1912 Sporting Runabout, one of the oldest surviving Morgans. It is powered by an 8hp, air-cooled, 964cc JAP engine. Below is the 1300cc Ford powered Buckland B3 of some 75 years later. Its 95bhp gave it a possible maximum of 130mph.

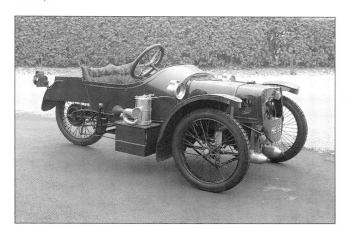

post-EC days, 425kg), they are treated as motorcycle-and-sidecar combinations. That is to say, you can drive a three-wheeler if you have only a motorcycle driving licence, you pay the same road fund duty as a motorcycle and can even drive unaccompanied on a provisional licence. There remains a surprisingly strong market for three-wheelers among ex-motorcycle owners who have never passed their car test.

Light weight is the final major category. Losing a wheel and its suspension components saves a few more vital pounds in the effort to keep a sports car's weight as low as possible. This is how the Morgan Super Sports remains so competitive on the track even today and it's the reason why there have been so many sports designs with three wheels.

Even where the law does not give three-wheelers a tax edge, you can still find three-wheelers. As this book aims to show, three-wheeling is a global phenomenon. From India with its motorised rickshaws to France with its microcars, from the styling houses of Europe to the supertrikes of the United States, there is a lively sub-culture devoted to three-wheeling.

That sub-culture has always been on the fringes of the motoring world. In many ways, trikes have more in common with motorbikes than cars. Traditionally, the British motoring press has ignored three-wheelers, while the motorcycle magazines have at least devoted regular coverage to them. In the earliest days, trikes could be found reviewed in *The Light Car & Cyclecar* magazine (*The Light Car* survived into the 1950s), while motorbike graduees read about them in *The Motor Cycle* or *Motor Cycling*. Even today, if you want to know about three-wheelers, read *Motor Cycle News* or *Scootering*.

People often think of trikes as machines owned by those who are unable to drive anything better, or

EXAMPLES OF THREE-WHEELER LAYOUTS

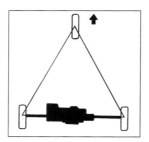

Single Front Wheel – Rear Engine/Rear-Wheel Drive eg. Bond 875

Weight distribution severely towards rear.
Traction very good.
Handling characteristics: Massive oversteer at limit. Rear end breaks away.

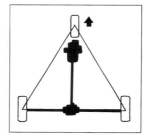

Single Front Wheel – Front Engine/Rear-Wheel Drive eg. Reliant Robin

Weight over steering front wheel.
When cornering, weight is thrown sideways and has nothing to stabilise it.
Handling characteristics: Understeer. At limit, rear wheel lifts and car in danger of overturning.

Single Front Wheel – Front Engine/Front-Wheel Drive eg. Bond Minicar

Rare configuration with weight over steering front wheel. Cornering forces throw weight sideways into empty space.
Handling characteristics: Understeer. Rear wheel prone to lifting and car in danger of overturning.

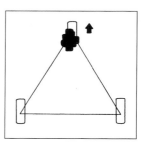

even as the exclusive transport of disabled people. How wide of the mark that is! Three-wheeler owners are as broad a group as any branch of the motoring world. You will find record-breaking sportsmen, devoted enthusiasts, idealists and family owners just as easily as the motorbike licence holder and impecunious driver.

Having three wheels is in fact specifically well-suited to a sports car format, and is correspondingly poor in load-carrying applications – although there have been many examples of utility trikes and even off-road trikes.

There is a right way to design three-wheelers, and a wrong way. Any three-wheeler design forms a triangle between the centre points of each wheel. Where you put the weight is crucial to the design's stability. The greater the proportion of weight over the single wheel, the more unstable is the vehicle. Conversely, place as much of the weight between the paired wheels and you have greater stability.

One of the best layouts was the Morgan. The engine sat virtually as far forward as possible, between the two front wheels. In cornering, the weight is thrown against the outside front wheel, which digs in. There is no reason why this should be any less stable than a four-wheeler.

One of the worst layouts was the notorious Reliant. Here, the engine (and therefore a large proportion of the weight) was sited immediately behind the single wheel which is, to compound its ignominy, positioned at the front of the car. When cornering, the weight is thrown sideways against thin air. With nothing to check it, it pulls the opposite edge of the car up, and you lift a rear wheel or, if you've really stepped in it, you topple right over.

Single Rear Wheel – Front Engine/Rear-Wheel Drive eg. Morgan

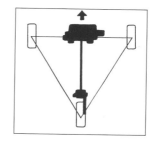

Traditional configuration. Weight predominantly at front, therefore in cornering, weight is thrown on to one of the front wheels for safe cornering.
Handling characteristics: Understeer at first, then at limit oversteer, with front wheel liable to lift.

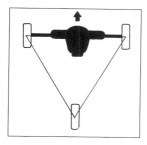

Single Rear Wheel – Front Engine/Front-Wheel Drive eg. Lomax

Configuration found in Mini based and Citroen 2CV based trikes. Weight between front wheels, therefore safer roadholding.
Handling characteristics: Understeer. At limit, front wheel may lift, but will lose power and return to road surface.

Single Rear Wheel – Rear Engine/Rear-Wheel Drive eg. Grinnall Scorpion

Weight towards rear wheel, but technically mid-engined. In cornering, weight is thrown sideways into empty space, but front wheels are unlikely to lift as rear end breaks away first.
Handling characteristics: Severe oversteer at limit. Wide rear tyre preferable for maximum grip.

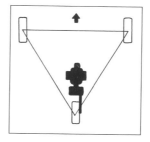

Generally speaking, two wheels at the front is more stable than one. At the back it doesn't matter as much if there is only a single wheel, even when the weight is shifted more towards the rear. Many trikes with admirable cornering abilities have an engine mounted close to the single rear wheel (as an example, go and drive a Grinnall Scorpion).

Other trikes have refined their stability by adding roll-bars, fattening the tyres or developing their suspensions. A couple have even had bodies which lean into corners like motorbikes! Interestingly, Morgan owners believe their cars to be safe handlers because the tyres are so *thin*. This means that, as the limit of traction is reached, the car begins to slide. With many modern rear-drive trikes carrying car rather than motorbike tyres, roadholding may be improved, but at the expense of handling: the front tyres continue to grip to such an extent that, when the power to the rear wheel becomes too great, the outer front wheel can lift and you are in danger of losing control or even flipping over completely. With narrow tyres, you tend to slide before lifting a front wheel, giving you more warning of imminent danger. Alternatively, if you have a front-wheel drive trike like a Lomax or a Mini-based car, lifting a front wheel will simply mean that power is lost to that wheel, and so the wheel returns to terra firma.

That is the case for the defence. In their favour, trikes are individual, often allowing for tremendous innovation in design. Likewise, the three-wheeler owner tends to be an individual, with an independent, unprejudiced and open mind. He – or indeed she – *knows* what the three-wheeler offers him, and often regards it as far superior to two-wheelers and four-wheelers. It all depends on your priorities.

In conclusion, the thing that draws all three-wheelers together is that they offer something different, something outside the normal frames of reference for conventional motor cars. Trikes have remained a consistent part of the motoring scene from Day One. But there is more to it than that. Far from being the oft-quoted 'missing link' between motor bike and motor car, three-wheelers can in fact be said to be the true fathers of modern motoring.

SOME OTHER MORE BIZARRE LAYOUTS

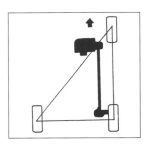

Scott Sociable (1921)

The front and offside rear wheels were aligned. The engine sat outside the triangle created by the three wheels – possibly the most unstable layout ever seen.

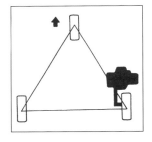

Gordon (1954)

The engine was mounted outside the bodywork in a special 'blister'. Again, an extremely unstable layout.

BMW Isetta (1957)

Once again, the engine is outside the triangle. According to how the car was loaded, stability was extremely variable.

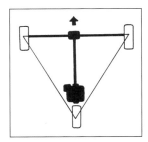

Arrowhead (1936)

The only example I have ever come across where a rear-mounted engine drives the front wheels. And it was a V8!

Chapter 1

Early Years

In the beginning man invented the wheel. He rolled his bluestone megaliths over logs, he tied his bronze age wagons to his oxes, and at a certain point he did a Fred Flintstone and created a wheeled device powered by his own legs. In all cases, the number of wheels would have been two or four. But never three.

Come the age of steam and things changed. At last man could travel using an engine! Arguably the first ever self-propelled vehicle (other than a railway engine) was a three-wheeler: a French military engineer by the name of Nicholas Cugnot built a cumbersome steam-powered machine as early as 1769, and it had a single front wheel. With an immense boiler slung right out in front, it was, however, wildly uncontrollable and, after the inventor crashed into a wall, he was jailed by the authorities.

The very first internal combustion car was also a three-wheeler. Karl Benz's pioneering prototype chugged off its blocks in 1885, launching the age of internal combustion on wheels. In its first drive, it suffered the same fate as Cugnot's steam carriage by driving into a wall. That was an aberration, however: the Benz would be the first car ever to enter production.

In this pioneering era, three wheels were adopted by Benz as the simplest and lightest means of transport. His prototype petrol engine was a four-stroke single-cylinder water-cooled effort which developed less than 1bhp at all of 250rpm! By the time the true production version arrived in 1888 – known as the Benz Patent-Motorwagen – its engine boasted 1.5bhp for a top speed of 10mph. Unfortunately, self-propelled vehicles had been banned in Benz's home region in 1887, so selling his cars proved rather difficult.

Benz staunchly followed the three-wheeler format while others, notably his arch rival Gottlieb Daimler, were using four. But while the trike offered advantages in power-to-weight ratio, the typically rutted roads of the day made their use less comfortable than four-wheelers, which could run smoothly through the

Probably the first self-propelled road vehicle: the immense steam-powered chariot of military engineer Nicholas Cugnot was born in 1769. It was completely uncontrollable.

The car which launched the motoring age: Karl Benz's 1885 three-wheeler used a rear-mounted single-cylinder water-cooled engine.

dreadful ruts when the central wheel of Benz's chariot bumped along unhappily over the rough centre of the road. Benz himself switched to four wheels in 1894.

Another man who contributed much to the early development of the car was the French Count De Dion. His first vehicle, a steam-powered three-wheeler built in 1883, became the basis of the great road cars constructed by De Dion in years to come. De Dion's pioneering tricycles – produced between 1896 and 1902 – with their high-speed engines and revolutionary suspensions, were much copied, notably by Humber in Britain.

Alongside De Dion, Leon Bollee was one of the fathers of the French motor industry. His first *voiturette* (a term he coined himself) appeared in 1895 as a 650cc engined three-wheeler with tandem seating for two. In its day, it was the fastest road car around. It inspired the design of many other machines but even Bollee realised the limits of its potential and had turned to larger four-wheelers by 1903.

In Britain, things took a little longer to get off the ground, largely because of the infamous Road Locomotives and Highways Act, which limited the top speed of self-propelled machines to 4mph and required a man to walk in front of the machine with a red flag to warn of its impending arrival. Probably the first ever British road car was a three-wheeled device called the Butler petrol cycle. Patented by Edward Butler in 1887 and completed around 1890, it was a twin-cylinder vehicle with twin steering front wheels. Butler was one of those inventors frustrated by the restrictive attitude of the government and he soon abandoned it with more than a hint of acerbity for the attitude of the authorities.

The infamous Act was not repealed until 1896 in the so-called Emancipation Act, after which there was a flurry of British activity. Three of the very first British cars, all trikes, arrived in that year: the Knight, the Pennington and the Wolseley.

The Knight was almost certainly the first true British car. It shared many features in common with the Benz, but had tiller rather than wheeled steering. E.J. Pennington's Torpedo Autocar was really nothing more than two motorised bicycles joined together. It was the subject of grandiose advertising (a picture

This was the world's first ever car advert, for the production version of Benz's three-wheeled 'Patent-Motorwagen' in 1888.

appeared with no less than nine people on it!), but the project suffered from a string of misfortunes at the hands of its inventor.

Some examples: Pennington claimed his tyres were unpuncturable, but his car had to retire from the 1896 London-Brighton run with... a punctured tyre. He said his engine would run on paraffin, but he faked a demonstration, using the best-grade petroleum instead. An English entrepreneur reportedly paid some £100,000 for Pennington's patents, which proved virtually useless.

Above: Rover was born here: this is an electric trike built in 1888 by J.K. Starley, who went on to found Rover in 1896. Below: Confidence trickster Edward Pennington on his Torpedo trike of 1896. One advert showed nine people on this slender machine!

Despite having used up literally millions of pounds of investors' money, it is doubtful whether more than 20 Penningtons of any description were ever produced.

The Wolseley was altogether more serious, the first design of Herbert Austin. Based on the layout of the Leon Bollee, it featured a flat twin engine and an overhead camshaft. Production did not truly begin

until 1899, and then with four wheels, but it was a good example of a three-wheeler blazing the trail for what would become a large manufacturer. Other famous British firms whose first forays were trikes included Singer, Humber, Riley and Lagonda.

During the Edwardian days, there was only really one type of customer: the rich. Consequently, three-wheelers were very marginal, with only a few types of the so-called tri-car actually entering production. Apart from these simple devices, most cars of this era were large, expensive and four-wheeled.

One popular British exception was a range of vehicles derived from the Autocarrier, a commercial tricycle. The name was shortened to the now-celebrated sigil AC for the passenger version, the AC Sociable. It sold for a remarkably low £100, while offering slightly more in the way of bodywork than its rival, the Morgan.

The roll-call of names active in the boom period before World War One included AC Sociable, Morgan, Condor, Girling, Jackson and many others in Britain alone. All were very crude and basic machines, only the Morgan having any pretence at sporting prowess. Ironically, the first car which Morgan founder, HFS Morgan, ever drove was a Benz rented from a Hereford dealer. He crashed it on his maiden voyage – very expensively – but the bug was firmly planted: see Chapter Two for the full Morgan story.

World War One decimated the ranks of car producers such that, at the declaration of armistice, only a tiny clutch of manufacturers were in a position to offer three-wheelers. The true glory years of the three-wheeler did not occur until after the war. By that time, the notion of motoring for the masses had become a genuine reality: cyclecars were a familiar sight, the Ford Model T offered cheap, reliable 'real' car transport and the first motorbikes were proving popular, too.

Three-wheelers slotted in at the base end of the motor car scale, just above motorbike-and-sidecar combinations. Bikers who were tired of the discomfort, the lack of weather protection and the unsociable nature of their beasts could graduate to the comparative luxury of a three-wheeler. Consistently, trikes represented the cheapest route into car ownership for bikers. A Morgan could be bought for as little as £80 at the zenith of its cheapness, while cruder machines such

Above: The Lagonda marque was founded in 1897 to build these three-wheelers. These were typical of the so-called 'tricar' made during the Edwardian years.

Below: The French-built La Va Bon Train was made in 1900 and used an 8hp De Dion single-cylinder engine.

Above: The famous British AC marque began life with the Autocarrier, a delivery van with three wheels. The passenger version was called the AC Sociable, and this example dates from 1910.

Right: The unbelievable Leyat Heliocycle was conceived by Frenchman Marcel Leyat. Yes, it was powered by a huge propeller. This 1914 prototype had three wheels but, after some spectacular accidents, finally went into production with four wheels.

as the JMB and Coventry Victor were even cheaper.

The economic conditions were right for a boom of sorts in the early 1920s, although the days of the cyclecar era would never be matched. Typically, manufacturers starting up in the post-war era lasted only a couple of seasons at the most.

There were exceptions. The Castle Three was unique in attempting to mate big car looks and equipment with the economy of three wheels, although it was too expensive to make much impact. Other trikes were successful because they were so cheap, like the Scott Sociable, the Harper and the Coventry-Victor. But by 1922, they had a new force to contend with: the Austin Seven, which rendered most three-wheelers superfluous. Those which survived did so by supplying extreme economy of ownership.

One of the main advantages of running a trike was the rate of annual horsepower tax, introduced in 1921. While ordinary cars paid a levy according to their fiscal horsepower rating (which was determined by the surface area of the engine's pistons), three-wheelers were charged at a flat rate. So while the Austin Seven owner of 1922 would pay £8 per year (£1 per horsepower), the owner of a three-wheeler which weighed less than 8cwt (406kg) paid a flat £4 each year – a significant difference in those days.

The Light Car & Cyclecar magazine ran a survey of running costs in 1924 and concluded that, over 6000 miles, a Morgan three-wheeler would cost £54, while an Austin Seven or a Jowett would require £65, and a Rover 8 some £68. These were big differences and largely explained the boom in three-wheeler sales.

There was always fierce controversy about three-wheelers. There was correspondence in the motoring magazines about the "beastly" tricycles, which held up faster cars on the rudimentary road system. Many felt that trikes were unsafe, but such comments usually came from manufacturers of four-wheelers who faced what they saw as unfair competition from tax laws which favoured trikes. Topping it all, three-wheelers were banned from racing against four-wheelers by the B.A.R.C. in 1921 and by the J.C.C. at Brooklands in 1924, on the grounds that they were dangerous. In the case of the Morgans, the real reason was probably that they were doing rather too well, a fact proven by a Morgan's emphatic win against Rileys, Austins and Amilcars after the ban was lifted in 1928.

Three-wheelers also found some favour abroad, although in smaller numbers because the same tax advantages were rarely duplicated. In France, once the *voiturette* craze had faltered, there remained a

We couldn't resist including this dinosaur from 1912. It is quite the largest tractor we've ever seen. Three-wheeled tractors continued to be popular in the USA until quite recently.

This an Eagle Tandem, with owner HFS Morgan at the wheel – his first-ever car. This British-made 8hp De Dion engined two-seater provided the inspiration for the first Morgan trike.

couple of interesting Morgan rivals, in addition to the French-licensed Morgan itself (the Darmont). These were the D'Yrsan (often claimed to return even better performance than the Morgans), and the Sandford, built by an ex-patriot Englishman in Paris. Both were current throughout the 1920s, while the Sandford lasted until the outbreak of World War Two.

In Germany, trikes were popular in the pre-1914 years, with machines like the Phanombil, Magnet and Tourist. Such economy three-wheelers became popular again with the onset of the economic depression of the late 1920s and early 1930s. Typically these were rather crude and unattractive devices with single driven front wheels.

By contrast, Americans avoided three-wheelers like the plague. There were many instances of cycle-type cars, but three-wheelers were always a rarity. When they did appear, they were usually large, heavy and fitted with large engines, as for instance in the Lewis Airmobile and Wagenhals.

Even further abroad, in Japan, just as the British car industry was founded on the experience gained with the earliest three-wheelers, so two Japanese giants began with tripeds. Mazda began making motorcycles and graduated to 'bike-derived trike trucks in 1931. Daihatsu's first foray into vehicles was in 1930 with a three-wheeler which became the firm's mainstay for more than 20 years. Its first car, the Bee, was launched in 1958 as a four-door, three-wheeled saloon with a 540cc rear-mounted air-cooled engine.

In Britain, the three-wheeler craze had effectively died by the mid-1930s. The economy models were having an impossible time competing with the new

B.S.A. de Luxe Model

Fabric body. Folding hood with envelope. Model T.W.1
Adjustable seat with hinged seat back giving
access to luggage compartment. Pneumatic
upholstery for seat.   £125

Only
£4 Tax
but
9 h.p. Engine

Three
Speeds
and
Reverse

Electric
Starter

The B.S.A Three Wheeler

is a fast car designed to meet the public demand for more comfort and
protection than is available from a motor-cycle, but is faster, lighter,
simpler and less costly in upkeep than the orthodox small car.

It is a three wheeler, with the drive in front. The front drive has the
following advantages :—

1. It concentrates the whole of the mechanism under the bonnet, where
   it is readily accessible.
2. It prevents skidding and makes the car very fast and safe at corners.
3. It minimises tyre wear by comparison with single wheel drives.

One reason why the B.S.A. is a three wheeler and under 8 cwts. is in order that its
Tax Rating may be only £4, although it has a 9 h.p. engine. The rear wheel to this car
is merely a trailing wheel, carrying a brake. All the wheels are quickly detachable
and interchangeable.

One of the most important features of the design of the B.S.A. Three Wheeler is that
it incorporates car type controls ; it has a reverse in addition to three forward speeds ;
it has a pedal accelerator ; the ignition timing and the slow running adjustment of the
throttle are on the steering column ; the pedal brake acts on all wheels and the hand
brake acts on the rear wheel.

The steering itself is extraordinarily good. In fact, this little car is a delight to drive
and its many virtues cannot possibly be appreciated without a trial.

*Perhaps the Morgan's greatest competitor was the BSA,
whose main difference was front-wheel drive. Its advert
cryptically stated that it had 'pneumatic upholstery'...*

*Coventry-Victor was another Morgan rival, selling
mainly on price. Produced between 1926 and 1938, it
came from a Coventry firm better known for its small
proprietary engines.*

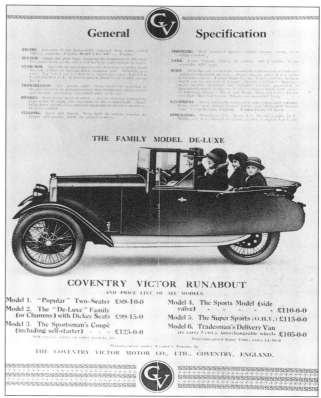

General   Specification

THE FAMILY MODEL DE-LUXE

COVENTRY VICTOR RUNABOUT

AND PRICE LIST OF ALL MODELS.

Model 1. "Popular" Two-Seater £89-10-0
Model 2. The "De-Luxe" Family
(or Chummy) with Dickey Seats £99-15-0
Model 3. The Sportsman's Coupé
(including self-starter) - - - £125-0-0

Model 4. The Sports Model (side
valve) - - - - - £110-0-0
Model 5. The Super Sports (O.H.V.) £115-0-0
Model 6. Tradesman's Delivery Van
(to carry 5 cwt.), interchangeable wheels £105-0-0
Puncture-proof Inner Tube, extra £1-10-0

Manufactured under Weaver's Patents by
THE COVENTRY VICTOR MOTOR CO., LTD., COVENTRY, ENGLAND.

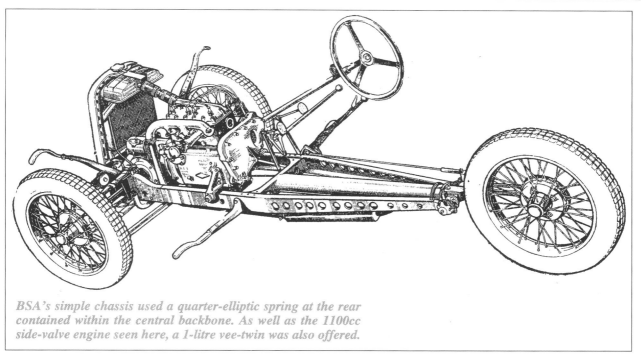

*BSA's simple chassis used a quarter-elliptic spring at the rear
contained within the central backbone. As well as the 1100cc
side-valve engine seen here, a 1-litre vee-twin was also offered.*

This extremely elegant and rather large three-wheeler was built by Frenchman Victor Bouffort in 1945, using a Citroen Traction Avant as its base. It had hydropneumatic suspension.

strain of mass-produced 'proper' small cars, spearheaded by the Morris Minor, which cost just £100 in 1931. In response to Morris, both Austin and Ford very quickly began offering £100 cars. At a time when the cheapest and crudest trike was being sold for £75 (probably at a loss in order to compete), three-wheelers stood little chance in the price battle.

Even the sporting three-wheelers like Morgan and BSA stood little chance. A new breed of cheap sports cars, led by the excellent MG M-Type Midget, eroded the giant-slaying reputation of the lightweight trikes, proving that four-wheelers could do a similar job for around the same outlay. The final nail in the coffin was the announcement in 1936 that Road Fund Tax would be abolished on all cars, effectively ending the edge on running costs traditionally enjoyed by three-wheelers. Just before the announcement, both Morgan and BSA introduced four-wheelers and that was basically the end of it.

Only Morgan (see Chapter Two) was making three-wheelers by the time of the outbreak of World War Two. After the war, too, the sole manufacturer of three-wheelers in Britain was Morgan, and that was on a very limited scale. Morgan was not joined by any other three-wheeler manufacturers in Britain until Bond in 1949, and that was a very different type of three-wheeler – an economy car along the lines of the microcars popping up all over continental Europe at that time. And their story is told in full in Chapter Three.

Chapter 2

The Morgan Story

If there is one car which sums up everything about why people love three-wheelers, it is the Morgan. It has all the attractive elements of three-wheeling but very few of its shortcomings. More than this, the Morgan is in many ways the pinnacle of the art, a trike which has still not been bettered. One has only to look at the number of Morgan imitations to appreciate the degree of respect in which it is held.

The Morgan was one of the original trikes, it lasted longer in production than any other British three-wheeler and was one of the best-selling of all time. Yes, it was a car born of economical considerations, but it became the very essence of sporting prowess. It turned the frowned-upon three-wheeled format into a force to be reckoned with on the road and on the track, while at the same time remaining a charming, no-nonsense, true grit sort of car.

Above: HFS Morgan (in the driving seat) proves the Morgan's mettle at Arkengarthdale Hill in 1911. Success at such events brought Morgan a lot of excellent publicity. Below: The very first Morgan, as shown at Olympia in 1910, had a single seat, tiller steering and almost no bodywork.

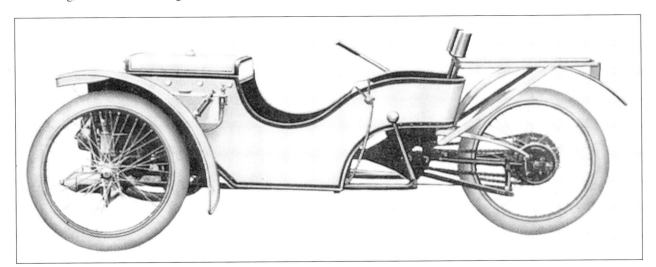

Above: The 1913 Sports Runabout which scored numerous successes in trials events.
Below: This 1912 four-seater prototype evolved into the popular Family model in 1915.
Opposite: This signed magazine cover celebrates HFS Morgan's historic one-hour sprint at Brooklands in 1912, when he achieved an average of just under 60mph. In the top hat is Prebendary H. George Morgan, HFS's father.

The Cyclecar

4TH DECEMBER, 1912
ONE PENNY.
Registered at the G.P.O. as a News

"Nearly 60 miles in one hour"

MORGAN MOTOR COMPANY LIMITED
PICKERSLEIGH ROAD, MALVERN LINK, WORCS. ENGLAND

F. H. Douglass   Morgan Agents
1A, SOUTH EALING ROAD, EALING, LONDON

Above: Early Morgan Sports were extensively raced by private owners, frequently trouncing far more sophisticated four-wheelers. Below: Simplicity itself: the twin-rail chassis doubled up as exhaust pipes! Also visible are the sliding pillar front suspension and simple bevel box and rear chain drive.

The Morgan was born when motoring was becoming more established. Harry Morgan (more commonly known as HFS Morgan) was the son of a vicar, a draughtsman with the Great Western Railway and a lover of the motorised horseless carriage. His interest in cars truly began with the purchase of an Eagle Tandem trike, leading him to set up garage premises in Malvern in 1906.

His very first design was completed in 1909, a basic single-seater three-wheeler with tiller steering and – in a historic first and last for Morgan – sliding pillar suspension with coil springs.

A year later, at the 1910 Olympia Cycle and Motorcycle Show, Morgan presented his first commercially available models. These were still single seater trikes of a very basic layout. Both had JAP engines (one a 4HP single-cylinder, the other an 8HP vee-twin). They were extremely simple machines, consisting of an absolute minimum of bodywork atop a twin-rail chassis and tiller steering. The Morgan was priced very low at 85 guineas, and it attracted much attention in those pre-Model T Ford days. Even Harrods was impressed enough to became an agent.

The tubular ladder chassis' side rails also acted as the exhaust pipes for the vee-twin engine, a set-up which was to remain a familiar feature of Morgan trikes for many years. Morgan's use of sliding pillar and coil spring front suspension was patented in 1910 (and is in fact still in use today by the Malvern manufacturer).

Power from the exposed vee-twin engine was transmitted by propshaft to a bevel box, and thence via chain to the rear wheel – simplicity itself. Two speeds were selectable, with no reverse on offer (although later after-market specialists supplied reverse gear adaptors).

But things did not really get going until 1911, when the number of seats grew to two and tiller steering was abandoned in favour of a conventional steering wheel, albeit still operating directly on the front wheels. The Morgan Motor Company was duly formed in 1912 – and the name remains the same even today. Using the money provided by his parson father (who became chairman of the new company), HFS Morgan expanded his Malvern garage to become a manufacturing works, having failed to gain any support for produuction from an established manufacturer. Morgan in those days was but one of a throng of such manufacturers, all selling their cyclecars in what was a tremendously popular market at that time.

What made the Morgan stand out? Above all else

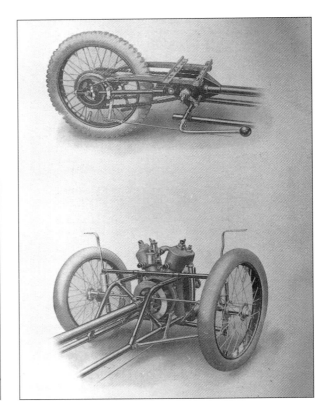

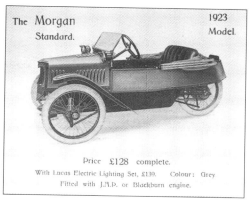

Above: The Morgan works at Malvern in 1920 at full pelt, producing some 50 cars per week. The same factory still makes Morgans today. Top right: This was the absolute basic model in 1923: a short-chassis two-seater with a JAP side-valve engine. Right: The more sporting Grand Prix, first seen in 1914, celebrated Morgan's historic victory in the Cyclecar Grand Prix. Below: Four seats in the Family model, which proved extremely popular with sprog-bearing ex-bikers. This is a 1926 model.

Above: With the Aero model, Morgan exploited the marque's considerable standing in sporting circles. It had a vee-screen and pointed tail. Below: In 1925, H. Beart drove this special-bodied Blackburne-engined Morgan at nearly 105mph – making it the fastest unsupercharged car in the world at that time. Opposite: When it arrived in 1928, the Super Sports model was in the vanguard of performance cars: 80mph was easily attainable and a string of records fell in its wake.

in those pioneering days, it was proven to be *reliable*. In trials events, it scored notable wins, like HFS Morgan's gold medal in the 1911 London-Exeter-London Trial, the first of ten such medals in this event. A Morgan won the first cyclecar meeting at Brooklands in 1912, smashing the speed record with a top speed of over 57mph. Perhaps most importantly, the Morgan beat off Bedelias, Violet Bogeys, GNs *et al* to win the coveted 1913 Cyclecar Grand Prix at Amiens in France. Morgans were making their mark – and demand soared.

In celebration of its French victory, Morgan launched the Grand Prix model in 1914. This was the first overtly sporting Morgan, with bodywork inspired by the car which won the 1913 event. It was easily distinguished by its high scuttle line and lack of bonnet sides.

The number of models quickly proliferated. In addition to the Grand Prix and the standard model, there next arrived a Family four-seater in 1915, based on a long-wheelbase chassis and with a pair of rather exposed seats behind the front pair. Then came the Sporting model in 1918, fitted with an air-cooled MAG engine and, the same year, a De Luxe (which basically meant it had a door!). These led a sales boom for Morgan, with production rising to as many as 50 a week in 1919.

Following World War One, a wide variety of engines was used – many now water-cooled instead of the traditional air-cooled units of the pre-vintage years. In addition to the most common JAPs, Morgans could be fitted with engines from Precision, Green, MAG, Anzani and, in the case of competition models, Blackburne.

On the re-opening of Brooklands, Morgans cleaned up in the three-wheeler classes. Numerous successes in trials, hillclimbs and cyclecar events served to spread

THE SPIRIT OF THE BIG RACING CAR!

NEW WORLD'S RECORDS

set up by Mrs. G. M. Stewart and Mr. W. D. Hawkes on the Montlhery Track, August 6th :—

5 Kilos at 113·52 m.p.h.=182·704 k.p.h.
5 Miles „ 107·51 „ =173·026 „
10 Kilos (from standing start) at 102·72 m.p.h.
 ==165·319 k.p.h.
10 Miles at 102·81 m.p.h.=165·456 k.p.h.

And at Arpajon on August 24th :—
FLYING KILO
at **115·6** m.p.h.
FLYING MILE
at **114·8** m.p.h.
(Subject to confirmation).

The MORGAN RUNABOUT Super-Sports Model at £150 is built to provide the exhilarating speed and power desired by the sportsman. It embodies a wealth of experience acquired at that great racing centre, Brooklands, and in important road events all over the world. The special O.H.V. engine will attain speeds up to 80 m.p.h. and can be tuned to considerably exceed this speed. Tax is only £4, and running and maintenance charges are proportionately low, giving total figures equivalent to those of the motorcycle and sidecar. The new MORGAN List giving particulars of all 1930 models may be had post free—write TO-DAY for a copy.

The Morgan Runabout

MORGAN MOTOR CO., LTD.,
MALVERN LINK, WORCESTERSHIRE

Above: The magnificent Super Sports was lower and lighter and came with a tuned OHV JAP engine as standard. Below: Rear view of a later Super Sports with its distinctive and elegant barrel back first introduced in 1934. Bottom: Among the changes for standard Morgans in 1932 were 3-speed gearboxes, dummy grilles, Dunlop Magna wheels and a rear-mounted spare.

the Morgan gospel still further and a new 38,400sq ft factory had to be opened to cope – at that famous address, Pickersleigh Road, Malvern. And a factory was opened in France for the manufacture of Morgans under licence: these were known as the Darmont. They gained something of a reputation as high-performance versions, as they could be bought with supercharged French-built Blackburne engines, and were capable of speeds up to 100mph.

But the development of the motor car was progressing fast. It was increasingly obvious that the cyclecar as a breed was doomed to extinction. With the arrival of the Austin Seven in 1922, there was no longer much reason to buy something which was basically inferior for about the same cost. The cheapest and crudest Morgan may have been cheaper than a Seven at £128 and the cost of running a trike may have been less, but with the far more sophisticated Austin Seven selling for only £165, there wan't much of a contest.

Cyclecar makers collapsed virtually overnight. Morgan survived because it was the best (indeed it long outlived the Austin Seven and all others of its ilk). This survival was due in large measure to the exploitation of its sporting distinction. With the long-tailed Aero (which first appeared in 1920), Morgan forged a profitable business with impecunious drivers who were attracted by the stunning speeds these machines could attain – usually in excess of 70mph. Aero models were identifiable by their V-split air deflector behind the radiator, streamlined tail and, typically, aero screens. For some

Above: New in 1935 was the F-Type, featuring a Ford Model Y side-valve engine, a new chassis and more enveloping bodywork. This is a two-seater model.
Below: The Ford engine of the F-Type brought a new era of refinement to the Morgan, and the model remained popular until its demise as late as 1952.

Above: This 1933 Sports Family with its 990cc Matchless engine is part of Chris Booth's impressive collection of Morgan three-wheelers, forming a part of his museum in Rolvenden, Kent.

Right: The F-Type had flowing wings, an opening bonnet and, in the case of this four-seater, opening doors.

time, it was offered only as a special-order model most often bought by customers whose main interest was racing. It always commanded a slight premium over its sister models (£150 in 1923, compared with £135 for a Grand Prix and £110 for a Standard model).

The Aero was offered with a variety of engines, including water-cooled side-valve and overhead valve units. From 1924, there was also a narrow-bodied single-seater version exclusively for racing. The cockpit was as stark as could be imagined and another distiguishing feature was an external exhaust pipe which ran under the scuttle. Aero models would also be offered with metallic lustre paint!

The Super Sports model which first arrived in 1928 boasted an enclosed, rounded rear end, cycle front wings and a low-level exhaust and was quoted as capable of up to 80mph. This became the seminal Morgan: it is the model the imagination always conjures up when the name Morgan is mentioned. It slotted in as the ultimate Morgan, costing some £145 in 1929 (compared to £110 for the Aero and £87 for a Standard). It was in Super Sports models that the most

celebrated speed records and competition successes were achieved.

Meanwhile, Morgan specials scored a string of record-breaking times, culminating in Harold Beart's 1100cc class record of 103.37 mph in 1926, a record which stood for some 40 years. Perhaps even more impressive was a one-litre unsupercharged JAP engined car driven by Gwenda Stewart in 1930: she broke the magic ton for an unbroken hour (when the record for *any* car was a mere 103.1mph – and that was done in a *supercharged* Cozette). Such exploits inspired many private owners to raise their racing driver aspirations by taking to the wheel of a Morgan in competitive events.

That is not to say that the standard models died out. Morgan continued to offer its economy models which competed keenly on price with the Austin Seven. The Standard and Family modles were supported by a large band of fiercely devoted owners who kept demand up to consistently high levels. The short-wheelbase Standard model, devoid of running boards, became one of the cheapest cars of its day during the 1920s, down to a mere £85 by 1928.

In the 1920s, Morgan's chief competition came from the Coventry-Victor and the French D'Yrsan. In the 1930s, there were also BSA and Raleigh to contend with, but none could match the brilliant career of the Morgan.

Changes were few during the life of the Morgan. Geared steering arrived as an extra in 1928, to become standard the following year. In 1931 came the first really major change of the Morgan's career: a conventional three-speed gearbox (plus reverse as well!) replaced the old two-speed bevel box, initially as an option but quickly as the standard item. Drive was still by chain and JAP engines were still favoured, although from 1933 990cc Matchless vee-twin units began to take precedence.

1935 marked something of a sea-change for Morgan. First there was a new model, the F type. The F stood for Ford, a nod to its use of the new 933cc side-valve four from the Model Y. There was an all-new body with much more enclosed bodywork mounted on a pressed steel chassis – and the luxury of a bonnet to

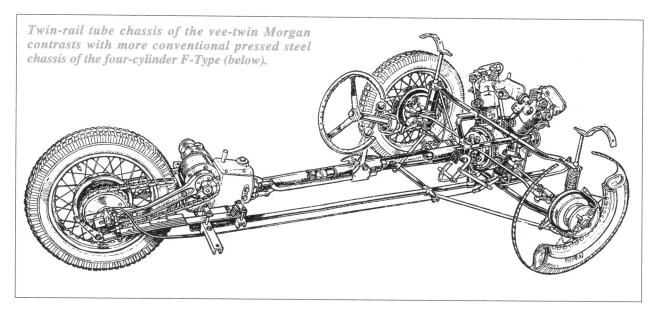

Twin-rail tube chassis of the vee-twin Morgan contrasts with more conventional pressed steel chassis of the four-cylinder F-Type (below).

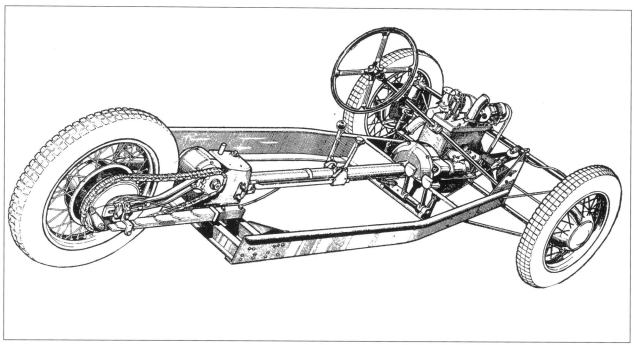

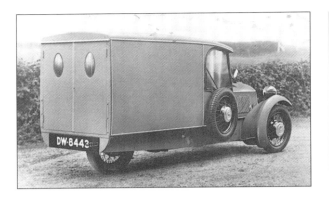

cover the engine! The main advantage of the F type was its smoothness over the vee-twins. Two models were available: the four-seater F4 and the F Super, with a two-seater body and different gearing. It became the new standard Morgan three-wheeler, while the old tubular chassis models took more of a back seat.

The F type could be said to have formed the basis of the second event of 1935 – an event which would change Morgan's fate. Yes, it was the unthinkable: a four-wheeler. For years, HFS Morgan had been vigilant in his defence of three-wheelers in the light of strong assaults from quadrupeds, and he maintained a constant correspondence in the motoring press. It may seem surprising therefore that he developed a four-wheeler during 1935 for launch in 1936. In fact, this was largely a response to the government's proposal to abolish the horse-power tax which had always treated three-wheelers so favourably.

The Morgan 4/4, the company's first four-wheeled effort, effectively took over the Malvern production lines. Production of trikes was down to just 29 in 1939, the last year in which the vee-twin models were listed, but manufacture of three-wheelers did continue in a very limited way after the war. A dozen Super Sports models were built up from spare parts, while the last F type was made in July 1952, some 42 years after the first three-wheelers appeared. Even then, production ceased only because Morgan was forced to concentrate on export markets, where the three-wheeler genre did not have the same taxation benefits enjoyed in Britain. It is estimated that approaching 40,000 Morgan trikes were built in those 42 years. After 1952, Morgan concentrated its efforts on its increasingly successful four-wheelers, which of course it continues to this day.

Top: This is a real rarity: a Morgan panel van of the type popularised by AC and Raleigh. Above: One-off special bodies on Morgan chassis tended to be geared towards lightweight racers. But here is an interesting closed coupe based on a vee-twin chassis. Below: The Morgan was built under licence in France by two separate firms, Darmont and Sandford. This is a 1929 Sandford which pre-empted its British forbear in its fitment of a four-cylinder engine, front brakes and a three-speed gearbox.

Above: Evocative replica, built in 1971, of the special-bodied Morgan raced by JAP experimental engineer EB Ware in the early 1920s. Below: Morgan Gránd Prix of 1922 alluded to the marque's success in the French Cyclecar Grand Prix in 1913 where it scored a resounding victory.

Above: Special-bodied Morgan built in 1933 and raced by Tommy Rhodes at the 1933 Relay Grand Prix at Brooklands. Right: One of the earliest surviving Morgans, a 1912 Sporting Runabout, fitted with an air-cooled 8hp 964cc JAP engine.

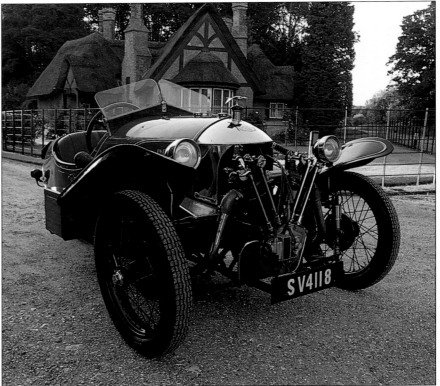

Left: Beautifully restored 1935 Morgan Family model with Matchless MX2 vee-twin engine. Below: Superb Super Sports barrel-backed model of 1934 used an air-cooled Matchless 990cc ohv air-cooled twin engine.

Right: Tiny Peel Trident was built on the Isle of Man from 1965 to 1966, seen here in the Manx Motor Museum. Below: Heinkel was conceived in Germany but was also made in England and Ireland, where the idea for this 'convertible bubble' was hatched.

Chapter 3

Bubblecars and Microcars

Ask someone to think of a three-wheeler and they'll almost certainly say "Reliant Robin". Ask them for a second example and they'll probably recall a bubble car. Bubble cars were probably the most successful users of the three-wheeled layout, which is to say they sold amazingly well – perhaps as many as half-a-million micro three-wheelers were sold in the 1950s.

Of course, almost all three-wheelers are of necessity small; but there are a few which have taken the word 'small' to undreamt-of bounds. The so-called microcar is a distinct and fascinating branch of the motoring tree of life, but it is extremely difficult to decide exactly what a microcar *is*.

Few would call the Reliant Robin or Triking 'microcars', and you can read about them elsewhere in this book. The microcars in this chapter are the genuine tiddlers, typified by the bubble cars of the 1950s. These are the cars which have engraved themselves on the memories of car enthusiasts as the 'real' microcars – cars which have three wheels not for fun, or for speed, or to exploit a quirk in the law, but for no other reason than to keep the design as simple as possible: to provide the absolute minimum necessary for travel by car. You only actually *need* three wheels, so why go to the trouble of designing a car with four?

As a breed, microcars have been around since the birth of the motor car, as evidenced by the designs detailed in Chapter One. In the austerity of the immediate post-war years, from 1945 to about 1960, microcars were in their element. The question of providing popular transport in the post-war years was heartily addressed by a large band of engineers across Europe – and even in America – by the creation of innumerable small cars.

The problem was that motoring in any form was very difficult following the war. If you were lucky enough to own a car, petrol was in short supply and was rationed in the UK well into the 1950s, so it was beneficial if you had the most economical car possible. Steel shortages also made car manufacture very difficult, and demand always far exceeded supply.

To a very large degree, British demand for miniature trikes blossomed at the expense of the motorcycle-and-sidecar combination. The rise of the bubble car was almost single-handedly responsible for decimating the popularity of motorbike combinations as family transport during the 1950s. Despite their crudity, microcars offered much more comfort than a

A scene from Dr Who and the Daleks or a line-up of early Messerschmitts? The car on the extreme right is a 1950 Fend Flitzer. All these cars are displayed at the celebrated microcar museum in Story, Germany.

Top: The early Messerschmitt KR175 had hemispherical front wings which looked very sci-fi but stopped the front wheels from turning! Above: The KR200 opened up like an oyster. Handling was very stable for a microcar. Note the handlebar steering.

motorbike and complete weather protection, all for similar running costs. The tax and licensing concessions granted to three-wheelers weighing less than 8cwt (407kg) also put the three-wheeled microcar on level ground with motorbikes.

The rich variety of cars which ensued included some brilliant designs like the Messerschmitt and Berkeley. It also brought about some of the most absurd creations ever seen on the road, the most obvious examples being the Isetta and Heinkel bubble cars.

Perhaps the most interesting of all was the Iso Isetta of 1953. This was the original 'bubble car', which spawned a whole gamut of similar looking spheroids. The commercial success of the bubble car, particularly in Germany and Britain – and of course its unconventional appearance – has led to it becoming synonymous with the microcar as a breed. Most continental bubbles were in fact four-wheelers, with very narrow-set rear tracks. But manufacturers like Heinkel and BMW-Isetta were quick to exploit the British market loophole with three-wheeled 'export' versions.

The momentum of the microcar movement was given a huge push with the first oil crisis of 1956, when the Suez canal became engulfed by war. Once again, fuel was in short supply and demand for small cars shot up: the bubble car truly experienced a boom.

But as the crisis eased, and as the average family's affluence steadily rose, the microcar began to look like an embarrassment. The arrival of brilliant new small cars like the Mini drove many off the roads. It was only the three-wheeled variety which retained any credibility in Britain during the 1960s, but by about 1966, the microcar was effectively dead. The Bond and Reliant continued as rather larger three-wheelers (see Chapter Four).

The theme did not die out completely. Or rather, it was revived in a most unexpected fashion in France during the 1970s. In France, the ground was exactly right for a spectacular rebirth of the true microcar – a type of vehicle even more crude and under-powered than the bubble cars of the 1950s. Just like most of the rest of Europe, France had laws allowing the freer use of transport with small engines. The French government said that anyone over 14 could drive a speed-restricted moped-engined vehicle (of up to 50cc) *without* the need for a driving licence or *matriculation*, the French version of the MoT. As a further concession, the vehicle didn't need to carry a registration plate and so didn't have to pay for a parking space.

A whole generation of strange and wonderful devices sprang up. They were all very small – typically around 7ft (2m) long – usually made from glassfibre and always rather bizarrely styled. Few could deny that these early French city cars were very crude, their little 50cc single-cylinder engines buzzing headily to reach a government-restricted top speed of 45km/h (27mph). If you passed the equivalent of a Highway Code test, you could graduate to one with a 125cc engine, in which case you were allowed whizz to the dizzy heights of 70km/h (44mph).

In the early days (from about 1973 to 1980), there were many three-wheelers on offer, selling in their thousands. But the increasing sophistication of the breed led to a trend for greater comfort and safety, and four-wheelers were preferred. The last French micro three-wheeler, the CEDRE, left production in about 1987.

To a certain extent, Italy followed the French experience, and several firms offered microcars very similar to the French *voiturettes*. Unlike in France, some survived until the end of the 1980s as three-wheelers, but the market was much more geared towards the old age pensioner and the vehicles remained crude to the end. Italian microcar manufacturers are now almost non-existent.

There have been a few attempts to launch updated microcars in Germany and Britain but these countries' laws are not as favourable to such cars: in Britain, a 16-year old could drive a three-wheeler with an engine of less than 50cc, but it still had to pass an MoT test and Type Approval regulations and the driver had to have a licence. The situation was even tougher in Germany. So the two big markets for microcars in the 1950s were the least active in the 1970s and 1980s.

If micro three-wheelers have a future, it is surely in the form of electric vehicles like the Danish-made City-El. A whole new breed of such zero-emissions vehicles is being created, with its centre in pollution-conscious Switzerland, where there are several futuristic-looking new electric three-wheeled designs on offer.

MESSERSCHMITT and FEND

The Messerschmitt is now regarded as one of the great microcars, to such an extent that the name is at least as familiar for its cars as it is for its aeroplanes.

The story begins with Fritz Fend, an engineer who worked for Messerschmitt during the war. At the end of hostilities in Germany, Messerschmitt ceased building aircraft, so Fend left the 'plane manufacturer to apply himself to road transport. He initially designed a string of pedal-powered three-wheelers and vehicles for veterans injured in the war.

The first road car as such was the Fend Flitzer of 1948, a desperately crude and tiny single-seater with the most basic specification imaginable: bicycle wheels and, in the first versions, pedal power. Those unable or unwilling to use their legs could opt for what was one of the smallest engines ever fitted to a motor car: a 38cc single-cylinder Victoria unit – powerful enough to take the 165lbs car to a heady top speed of 19mph. Unhurried drivers were rewarded by a claimed fuel consumption of 235mpg. Both enclosed and convertible versions were offered, the latter with a transparent inflatable ribbed hood!

The next Flitzer used motor scooter wheels and a 98cc Fichtel & Sachs engine

developing 2.5bhp, for a top speed of 38mph. In 1950 came the improved Kabinenroller, a marginally more substantial open or closed single-seater with lines even more portentous of the Daleks of *Dr Who*. It used a more robust 98cc Riedel engine (4.5bhp, 47mph). Fuel consumption was down to a 'mere' 100mpg. Fend had made around 282 motorised vehicles by the time he began his famous collaboration with Professor Willy Messerschmitt in January 1952.

Messerschmitt's factory had been forbidden from building any more 'planes after the end of the war, so he had devoted his works to the repair of railway rolling stock. He had always kept in touch with Fend and was an admirer of his ideas. Seeing his little three-wheelers, he went into partnership with Fend for the design of a small car. The first fruit of this get-together was the Rikscha, a bizarre 125cc three-wheeler where the driver sat as on a scooter behind a sort of scoop which could carry two passengers. It did not enter production.

More serious – and influential – was the first Kabinenroller. The very first models bore Fend's own name and were sold as the Fend FK 150 from early 1953. They had 148cc Fichtel & Sachs 6.5bhp engines mounted in the rear. Unlike most German microcars of the period, the Kabinenroller began life as a three-wheeler and remained a trike until the very end.

In March 1953, Messerschmitt announced that it would be selling the model under its own name with a larger 174cc Fichtel & Sachs engine, which

Messerschmitt KR201 was the cabriolet version with full folding hood. That gave you an extra way to get in by simply leaping over the sides.

established the classic form of all production Messerschmitts. It had many striking features, but the most celebrated was the Plexiglass canopy which resembled so closely the canopies of Messerschmitt's wartime aircraft – although they were *not* left-over aircraft items. The whole canopy swang up sideways to allow entry for two passengers, who sat in tandem in the narrow body (a small child could also just be squeezed on to the rear seat). A pair of bug-like headlamps provided illumination and the front wheels were enclosed in hemi-spherical wings. If science fiction had been a popular form in 1953, the Messerschmitt would surely have been greeted as an alien pod dropped from Planet Weird.

The production KR 175, as the car was known, had a 174cc Fichtel & Sachs single-cylinder two-stroke engine sited in its rump which pumped out 9bhp. Even with such little power, the lightness (460lbs) and aerodynamics of the 'Schmitt gave it a top speed of 56mph and established it as one of the 'performers' of the microcar scene. It was steered by a pair of handlebars which incorporated a twist-grip throttle. By the time it was replaced in 1955, 19,668 had been built.

Its replacement was the KR 200, whose engine had grown, as the name suggested, to 191cc and 10bhp. The body was slightly different, too: there were cut-outs in the front wings to allow the front wheels to steer more freely and so give something better than the appalling turning circle of the original KR 175. A floor-mounted accelerator replaced the old scooter-style twist-grip throttle and the 'Schmitt was also now able to go in reverse – by restarting the engine in the opposite direction, allowing for the terrifying possibility of travel in reverse in four gears!

World-famous Isetta bubble car as launched in Italy in 1953. BMW took over the rights to the Isetta in 1955 and made over 160,000 of them.

There were better interior appointments, including some rather unusual options. One show car appeared with mock-alligator skin upholstery, there was the option of a pretty chunky valve radio and you could even order a set of body mounts for luggage or even skis!

The KR 200 was a huge success: as the most professional microcar available in Germany, it was a best-seller. But there was now severe competition from other marques such as BMW, so Fend replied with some publicity stunts, like the antics of the high-speed streamlined KR 200 Super trike, which broke 25 class speed records in 1955 (top speed: 87mph).

On the commercial front, the appeal of the model was significantly extended by the arrival of a cabriolet version in 1956, dubbed the KR 201.

As a result of court action by Mercedes Benz, who obscurely claimed that Messerschmitt's 'flying bird' symbol looked too much like its own three-pointed star, the diamond-shaped FMR badge appeared on Messerschmitts from January 1957: this stood for Fahrzeug und Maschienenbau GmbH Regensburg. Get your teeth around that!

Without doubt, the Messerschmitt caught the bubble boom in full swing and was one of the more popular and attractive designs. It had its faults, like skittery road behaviour and lack of refinement – but it was better than most microcars by a quantum leap. Almost from the beginning, Messerschmitts had been making a loss for the parent company, which survived by making bottle top dispensers and continued the make the Kabinenroller as something of a labour of love.

The very last examples of the KR and its four-wheeled high-performance sister, the Tg500, left the Regensburg works in 1964, by which time over 30,000 KR 200s had been supplied. Apart from an abortive attempt at licensed production in Italy in 1954 (where the car was to be known as the Mivalino), that was that for the Messerschmitt.

ISETTA

The bubble car was born in Italy when a fridge manufacturer called Renzo Rivolta smashed his brave new egg on to the road. The year was 1953 and it must be said that the Italians were really not ready for driving themselves round in a metal spheroid like the Iso Isetta, which sold in the hundreds rather than in the factory farm-load. They preferred the small Fiat 500 and 600.

It was left for the German licensee BMW to cash in on the charms of the Isetta, which it did from 1955. In 1956 alone, BMW sold 22,543 examples – almost four times the total production of the Italian Isetta. Continental customers lapped them up.

German-market cars always came with four wheels

– the rear pair were set only 20 inches apart – and had BMW 247cc motorbike engines. For export markets, a 295cc 13bhp engine was fitted from 1956, in which guise the car was known as the BMW-Isetta 300, and it had three-wheels, a configuration developed specifically for export. As the engine was slung off to one side in the rear, that led to some interesting handling characteristics. In 1957 came a revised version with new 'one-piece' side glass which incorporated a sliding mechanism for ventilation; this replaced the three-window fixed glass inherited from the Iso.

The end of the BMW line was not reached until 1962, by which time the remarkable total of 161,728 BMW-Isettas had been built. It is amusing to recall that the giant which is BMW today was practically built on three-wheeled bubble cars – the first example of a truly mass-manufactured Bimmer.

In 1957, BMW sold a licence to produce the Isetta in Britain, where Isetta of Great Britain manufactured the model at a converted locomotive factory in Brighton – where there was no road access, all deliveries having to be moved by train! From 1957 to 1964, British Isettas were built in three- and four-wheeled forms, with saloon, convertible and pick-up bodies, at a rate of up to 175 per week. Estimates put the total quantity built in Britain at a remarkably high 20,000 to 30,000.

HEINKEL

Plagiarism or progression? Heinkel's bubble car was too close to the Isetta to be a mere co-incidence. But it was definitely not a straight copy: indeed the Heinkel

Above: Heinkel's bubble car was very similar to the Isetta, but had seating for four (just!) and a 175cc motor scooter engine. Below: Surely the least likely candidate ever for a delivery van? The Heinkel was built in England by Trojans, who offered this curious aberration in the mid-1960s.

Above: Lawrie Bond's first production car, the Bond Minicar. It was Britain's only three-wheeler when launched (1949) – with the sole exception of Morgan. Below: By 1952, Bond had progressed to the MkC stage which boasted an ability to turn 360°within its own length! Bottom: The MkF was the final shape of the Minicar from Bond, adding such luxuries as a 246cc engine and four-speed gearbox.

improved on the Isetta's concept in a number of areas.

Ernst Heinkel was the man behind the design of the Saab three-cylinder two-stroke engine and had developed a single-cylinder four-stroke for use in a motor scooter, which proved highly successful.

He used this same 175cc unit in his Heinkel Kabine Cruiser of 1956. Outwardly it resembled the Isetta (there was initially a lot of consternation from BMW), but that was superficial. The egg shape and opening front door were familiar, but the Heinkel did not use a folding steering wheel and was both lighter and prettier. It also had more space inside, even offering children's seats in the rear. And it was far more commonly produced as a three-wheeler (although a 204cc four-wheeler was also made).

Ernst Heinkel died in 1958, just after his little car was withdrawn from production in Germany with a little under 12,000 examples sold.

Like the Isetta, production continued for many years in other countries. In Argentina, the local Heinkel was built from 1957 to 1959, and 2000 examples were sold. In Ireland, where production transferred from Germany in 1958, the model was known as the Heinkel-I. Somewhere in the region of 8000 cars are estimated to have been built in Ireland until 1961, when the licence transferred to Trojans in the United Kingdom. The Irish firm had developed a full convertible version called the Open Tourer, although it was sadly not productionised.

The Croydon-based firm Trojan was perhaps most famous for its cheap but crude small cars which it made from 1922 until 1936. Its decision to take on the Heinkel marked its return to car manufacture. It made three-wheeled cars in left and right-hand drive form, from 1961, latterly with the name Trojan 200. Trojan also made an Estate Van version towards the end of the model's life. By 1965 it had become disenchanted with car production (including the Elva sports car range which it had also taken on) and the bubble was abandoned, after some 7000 cars had been made. The total number of Heinkels built therefore approached 30,000.

BOND MINICAR

Alongside Egon Brutsch, Lawrie Bond was one of the most prolific post-war microcar designers. Not only did he found his own marque – one of the first British post-war ventures – he designed or had a hand in a variety of other microcars, most notably the Berkeley and Opperman.

In 1948, Lawrie Bond had developed an extremely basic three-wheeled prototype as a form of cheap, popular transport. Wanting very much to put it into production, he began talks with Sharp's Commercials of Preston, Lancs and eventually they agreed to make

the car under Bond's name.

So the Bond Minicar was launched in 1949. One can realise just how basic the prototype was from the *improved* specification of the aluminium-bodied production car: it had cable and bobbin steering, a Perspex windscreen, open bodywork, no doors, brakes on the rear only and no rear suspension (the tyres were left to absorb all the bumps). A 122cc single-cylinder two-stroke Villiers engine sat immediately behind the single front wheel, driving it by chain through a three-speed gearbox.

These early Bonds were intended merely as runabouts but, such was the success of the model, many people wanted to use their Minicars as all-purpose transport. To oblige them, Bond also offered a larger 197cc Villiers engined version.

An improved model, the Minicar Mark B, arrived in 1951 with the luxury of rear suspension, but still no dampers! Like the Mark A, most production cars were two-seaters, although vans, Minitrucks and 2+2 Family Safety Saloons were also offered.

A door appeared for the first time on the Mark C of 1952 – on the passenger's side only. There was also now a front brake and better suspension. In appearance, the Bond also got front wings, making it look like a much larger car. One might dismiss this as pure puff, but the arrangement allowed the Bond for the first time to do a now-celebrated manoeuvre: the front wheel and engine could turn through 180 degrees, permitting the Bond to turn within its own length. By 1955, Bond was making 100 cars per month.

The Mark D (1956) shared the C's body but added 12 volt electrics. But the Mark E of 1957 marked a complete design overhaul. Now fitted with a chassis (as opposed to the stressed body with strengthening cross-members of the earlier models), the Bond was now strong enough to be fitted with full-size doors – on both sides of the car! The body looked much different, sporting a slab-sided profile and squarer lines.

As the weight of these more sophisticated Bonds was rising, Villiers was approached to build a bigger engine. Reboring the existing unit to 246cc provided an extra 4bhp and a 25% increase in performance; cars fitted with this engine were known as the Mark F (1958). A four-speed 'box was now standard.

In 1961, the Mark G added a few more refinements: a hard-top with a 'breezeway' rear window, larger (10in) wheels, hydraulic brakes and wind-up windows. An estate version (which Bond claimed to be "the world's first three-wheeled estate car") arrived shortly after, of which there was a Ranger van version.

Allard Clipper was a disastrous departure for the sports car maker in 1953. It is unlikely that it reached proper production.

The Minicar had been a very successful design – probably the most popular of any British microcar. But sales of the still very basic and slow car were declining so that, by 1966, production of the Minicar ceased. A total of just under 25,000 of all types had been built.

Since 1963, Bond had also been making a Triumph Herald based sports car called the Equipe. The experience gained in making its glassfibre body was put to use in the Minicar's 'replacement', the 875 of 1965 – a very different car, and not a true 'microcar'. The details of this three-wheeler are related in Chapter Four.

ALLARD

Alongside AC, Reliant and Bond, Allard was one of the few firms engaged in that peculiarly English practice of making microcars and sports GT cars both at the same time. In Allard's case, most opinion remains that they should have stuck to building sports cars.

The Clipper was very weird by any standards but it was also desperately crude. Introduced in October 1953, it was an oddly shaped glassfibre hardtop coupe – in fact, one of the first ever cars fitted with a plastic body. It was designed by David Gottlieb (who was later to design the Powerdrive) and looked like a pair of eggs given a styling job by Chevrolet. On some versions, there was even a dickey seat in the rear 'boot'.

The Clipper was a light car at just 6cwt (305kg). The engine was a 346cc Villiers 8bhp unit mounted in the rear and driving only one of the rear wheels. There were cooling problems and a driveshaft weakness, making it woefully unreliable.

The project lasted for only two years or so before

Sidney Allard pulled the plug on the project to concentrate on his sports cars, which were also then having trouble selling. Very few Clippers were ever made, true production thankfully never being reached. Today only three are known to survive.

BERKELEY

When the Morgan died in 1952, there was really no choice at all for the three-wheeler man who had a sporting inclination. To be honest, there would not really have been sufficient demand for such a vehicle during the 1950s. But by the end of the decade, sports cars were back on the agenda and into the breach stepped the amazing Berkeley. The three-wheeled version effectively became an updated Morgan.

Lawrie Bond, the prodigious microcar designer, instigated the car by approaching Charles Panter of

Berkeley Coachworks in 1955 with an idea for a new micro sports car. Previously, Berkeley had pioneered the art of glassfibre as early as 1948 in its caravans. Panter agreed and so Bond built three prototypes in 1956. The result was a tiny (10ft 2in) car of GRP unitary construction and independent suspension all round, weighing just 5.5cwt.

It took until 1959 for a three-wheeled version to appear. Panter decided to modify the rear end of the four-wheeled Berkeley Sports and create a three-wheeler called the T60, launched in August 1959. Why it took him so long is a mystery, but it was an instant smash hit, offering genuine sports car-like ability and handsome lines. With its 328cc Excelsior engine, a top speed of 60mph was possible with the sort of handling

Above: Attractive Berkeley T60 mated all the character of Lawrie Bond's four-wheeled sports car with the economy of three wheels.
Below: Even with a tiny 328cc Excelsior engine, the T60 was decidedly sporting in nature.

Berkeley Bandini. Unlike the original Berkeleys, these had a 30mm tubular steel space frame chassis but were set up to accept a Mini front subframe with any A-series engine from an 848cc Mini lump right up to a Metro Turbo. An alternative was to use motorbike engines (*a la* original Berkeley) driving through a modified Mini differential. The single rear wheel was attached to a specially-made swinging arm suspended on a coil/spring damper unit.

The only external difference from the 1960 T60 was the wheel arches, which had to be widened by $2\frac{1}{2}$ in either side to accommodate Mini wheels. However, you could radically alter your T60 lookalike with the option of D-Type style GRP head fairings, a blanked-off passenger's seat, a hard-top and early type or B95-style nose treatments. See Chapter 7 for the fully story of the reborn Berkeley Cars.

which was normally reserved for big sports cars (of the four-wheeled variety).

A true four-seater version was also made from 1960 under the name T60 Four. Squeezing four passengers into such a tiny space was near-impossible and performance must have suffered disastrously when fully-laden. The four-seater remained a rarity (only about 55 examples were sold), while the standard-issue T60 notched up nearly 1800 sales in just over a year – a remarkable total. Berkeley as a marque died in late 1960 after being faced by unsurmountable problems. At a time when the company's caravan making business had slumped dramatically and caravans were having to be stockpiled, it also suffered from a strike by its supplier of driveshafts, Hardy Spicer. Not surprisingly, Berkeley went bust as a result.

Most enthusiasts who have owned a Berkeley T60 would agree that it is one of the best three-wheelers ever made, although as parts became difficult for the cars, many were converted over to front-wheel drive Mini power. This had in fact happened even while the company was still operating.

In the 1990s, a Berkeley enthusiast called Andy Argyle came to light offering replacement chassis, GRP panels and bodyshells for Berkeley cars, including T60s. By 1993, his Berkeley Cars operation had entered full production with complete T60 Mini-based body/chassis kits, which were sold with the name

Above: One of the best three-wheelers ever made, the T60 was remarkably successful on the sales front: nearly 1800 were sold. Below: Even while Berkeleys were still leaving the factory, some owners were converting their cars to Mini power and adding flared wheel arches to cover the wider Mini wheels.

FRISKY

British born Captain Raymond Flowers was behind the unique Frisky project. His strange automotive career began in Egypt with the Phoenix sports car, the only car ever to wear the official Egyptian racing colour (purple – not a lot of people know that!). While in Egypt, he also designed a microcar prototype which he brought back with him to Britain in 1957.

It was initially given a redesign by none other than the celebrated Italian stylist Michelotti. Eventually the Frisky went into production with a second restyle, this time sporting American-style rear fins, no less! This was a four-wheeler with a very narrow-set rear pair of wheels requiring no differential. The model was named the Friskysport and put into production by Henry Meadows Ltd of Wolverhampton, who were then making engines.

A year later, in 1958, Captain Flowers decided to press ahead with a more basic Frisky, which he called the Family Three. This was Frisky's first three-wheeler and boasted accomodation for four people (just!), using 197cc and, from 1959, 246cc two-cylinder engines. Why Flowers had even bothered with a four-wheeled version in three-wheeler friendly Britain is not recorded, but whatever the reason, production

The Frisky was conceived as a narrow-track four-wheeler with sporty pretensions. It was quite fast – even stylish – for a microcar, but economy-oriented three-wheelers were more popular.

concentrated solely on three-wheelers after 1961. A larger three-wheeler, the Prince, was offered from 1960 with a 324cc or 328cc engine.

Both convertible and coupe versions were offered during the models' production life. The coupe's roof was perhaps rather too low, for with its hard suspension, passengers found their heads becoming bloodied on the roof! After its fourth successive change of premises, Meadows abandoned production of the Frisky in 1964.

PEEL

Despite its small size, the Isle of Man-based firm Peel Engineering was one of the fountains of the microcar garden, forever producing fresh ideas and new designs. Its main business was making glassfibre moulds for motorcycle fairings, boat hulls and so on, in which it was something of a pioneer.

In 1955, it was encouraged by the appearance of several GRP-bodied cars to enter the world of motor car manufacture. Its first project was the Manxman, a small three-wheeler with a steel tube chassis and an enclosed GRP body. Initially a rear-mounted 350cc Anzani two-stroke twin drove the single rear wheel by chain, but later a 250cc Anzani unit was fitted. A top speed of 50mph (80km/h) was claimed with a fuel consumption of 90mpg.

Two hammock seats were supplemented by a rear compartment which could carry two children or 16 cu ft of luggage. Entry was gained via a most unusual system: the semi-circular door pivoted at its rear base, swinging upwards and back, flush with the bodywork.

The plan was to sell the 4.5cwt Manxman in kit form for £299 10s, but it is very unlikely that proper production ever began. However, Peel did make several examples of its larger GRP bodyshell for Ford Ten chassis, called the P1000, which appeared in the late 1950s.

The car for which Peel is now most famous is the P50 of 1962. This was almost without doubt the world's smallest ever passenger car. In Peel's literature, it stated that the prototype measured just 4ft 2in (127cm) long, 2ft 9ins (84cm) wide, and 3ft 10ins (117cm) tall. Production cars were a slightly more portly 4ft 5ins (135cm) long and 3ft 3ins (99cm) wide, but they

Right: Undoubtedly the world's smallest production car was the Peel P50 from the Isle of Man, seen exhibited at Beaulieu. Only 4ft 5ins long, it was little more than a chair on wheels.

Left: About half of the entire car folded forward to allow entry to the brave passengers. Top speed was about 40mph. Below: Only marginally larger was Peel's Trident, a tiny two-seater with a bubble top. Nicknames included 'Clockwork Orange' and 'Policeman's Helmet'.

only weighed a mere 132lbs (60kg).

In prototype form, the P50 appeared with a single front wheel and twin rear wheels, but production models had the layout reversed. The P50 was essentially a single seat surrounded by a one-piece GRP box incorporating a single front headlamp. A DKW 49cc fan-cooled engine sat underneath the driver, where it chirped away in an extremely noisy fashion. It drove the single rear by chain via a three-speed gearbox.

The P50 was hardly a comfortable machine to drive and there were stabilising 'nodules' to the rear of the bodywork on some cars to stop them toppling over on corners, which was an inevitability even at speeds well below its maximum of 30mph. The provision for reversing consisted of a handle fitted on the back, the owner being expected to manhandle the car into a parking space. No two Peels were ever identical, being individually finished at the factory.

Still, at a price of £199 10s in 1963, many were tempted. New P50s were despatched in a wooden box which was designed to double up as a garage! Up to 1966, somewhere in the region of 75 cars were delivered, many of which still survive today.

Peel's next model was the Trident three-wheeler of 1965, which was larger than the P50, but only just (measuring 6ft or 183cm long). The GRP body of the Trident consisted almost entirely of a forward-hinging section which had a transparent Perspex dome as a roof and a flat glass windscreen. The umbrella handle-shaped Citroen DS-inspired steering column was also hinged and rose with the canopy.

The Trident could seat two side by side (just) or some were supplied as single-seaters with a shopping

Running the Peel a close second on size, the Brutsch Mopetta was claimed to be amphibious and was at one stage scheduled to be made by Opel!

basket beside. The engine was initially the same 49cc unit as the P50, but some cars had 100cc Vespa engines, which had to be kick-started to life using a detachable pedal. Stalling at the lights was a thing to be avoided, as it meant opening up the canopy, leaping out, fitting the starting handle in place and then jumping on it! With a turning circle of 8ft, there was really no need for a reverse gear, which is just as well since none was fitted. You got a handle on the rump instead.

Costing £189 19s 6d, the Trident was even cheaper and marginally more practical than the P50. It was advertised as being "almost cheaper than walking", having a consumption of about 100mpg. A four-wheeled electric version also appeared briefly in 1966. Peel stopped making the Trident in 1966, after selling about 45.

BRUTSCH

Egon Brutsch was one of the great microcar genii. He was a prolific creator of ideas. Not always sound, hardly ever sensible, and ultimately, without commercial success. Coming from a wealthy background, he could afford to do this.

Following a string of four-wheelers, his first three-wheeler project was the 200 Spatz ('sparrow'), which was presented at the 1954 Paris Salon. It was a smoothly shaped little open three-wheeler which looked sporting and attractive. However, it had no chassis, relying solely on the strength of the plastic shell to keep the mechanicals in place, and it was certainly not a monocoque! This was in the early days of glassfibre when the strengths of the material were often over-estimated: the 200 proved to be a very weak structure and cracked all over the place. A German judge even ruled that the car was illegal on this count! It later re-emerged as the much-modified, four-wheeled Spatz.

Brutsch then built the Zwerg ('dwarf') in 1955, which was made in one- and two-seater forms, the former with a 75cc engine, the latter with a 250cc Maico unit. About 16 were made of both types and more were built in France under the name Avolette.

The next three-wheeler project was the Mopetta of 1956, perhaps Brutsch's most celebrated car. The Mopetta can justifiably rival the Peel P50 as the smallest car ever built: only 67ins (170cm) long, 34.7ins (88cm) wide and 39ins (100cm) high. It weighed just 134lbs (61kg) and had a 49cc engine developing 2.6bhp, enough to give it a thumping top speed of 27mph (45km/h). In appearance it resembled an egg in the process of hatching its driver.

The original publicity preposterously stated that

the Mopetta could float in water. Nobody ever tried, which is perhaps just as well, since the engine sat exposed beside one of the rear wheels! Georg von Opel (late of Opel) was all set to produce the car in series as the Opelit, but the project came to nought, mainly because the German authorities refused to allow the contraption on the road. Most Mopettas therefore found homes through the British Brutsch importer.

A slightly larger sister, the Rollera, arrived at the same time, offering 98cc and a top speed of 50mph (80km/h); there was also licensed production in France.

Again in 1956, Brutsch presented his Bussard ('buzzard'), a trike which resembled to a large degree the original Spatz of 1954, although it did now have a steel tube frame! It used the familiar 191cc Fichtel & Sachs single-cylinder engine (as proven in the Messerschmitt). A mere total of 11 Bussards was built up to the end of Brutsch's manufacturing career in 1958.

Above: Brutsch's Rollera was only fractionally larger than the Mopetta and represented the most basic form of car transport in the 1950s. Below: The Brutsch Bussard of 1956 was the last three-wheeler made by the eccentric German inventor, Egon Brutsch. Several were sold in Great Britain.

Above: Bizarre telephone kiosk styling for the Scootacar, seen outside the locomotive factory of Hunsletts in Leeds. Below: Scootacar Mk2 of 1960 had revised front and rear styling and more interior space.

SCOOTACAR

The Scootacar was the only all-British attempt to produce a true 'bubble' car, as inspired by the Isetta and Heinkel, rather than just a microcar with three wheels. Even then, it came out looking decidedly odd, with an improbably tall (5ft) body which looked like it *had* to topple over on corners.

In fact, the Scootacar worked remarkably well in practice. The driver sat on the front end of a narrow tandem seat. A single passenger could sit astride the engine itself, rather like a motorcycle pillion, or two very friendly types could just squeeze in either side of it. Steering was by handlebars, which gave a very direct response and handling was better than might be imagined, as most of the weight did in fact sit quite low down.

The origins of the Scootacar, it is rumoured, began when the wife of the director of Hunslets, the railway locomotive makers based in Leeds, said she wanted something easier to park than her Jaguar. The Scootacar was certainly that: its length was only 7ft 7ins (231cm) and the whole thing weighed just over 500lbs (230kg), thanks to the light weight of its glassfibre bodywork.

The first Scootacars, made from 1958, came equipped with a Villiers 9E 197cc single-cylinder two-stroke, which produced all of 8bhp, delivering it by chain to the single rear wheel. Being fairly streamlined for this type of car, that was enough to power it up to a claimed 51mph.

In 1960 came the MkII De Luxe version which looked rather different, with a more bulbous front and an elongated tail. The seating arrangement was different, too: the driver now had a more comfortable individual seat and the rear passengers no longer needed to apologise for digging each other in the ribs: there was enough elbow room for all.

The twin-cylinder 16bhp 324cc Scootacar MkIII De Luxe Twin arrived in 1961, selling for a fairly hefty £50 premium over the MkII version. Perhaps it was this, combined with what must have been the sheer terror of driving a MkIII at its top speed of 68mph, which kept it from being popular. Of the 1000 or so Scootacars built in total, a mere 20 or so were the more powerful De Luxe Twin variety. Hunslets put a stop to Scootacar production in 1965.

'The World's Best Three-Wheeler' said the adverts for the Coronet at its launch in 1957. Few people got the chance to find out as only a couple of hundred were made.

CORONET

The Coronet represented an attempt to offer full-size car refinements in a microcar package. It was an open two-to-three-seater with a single rear wheel, in front of which its 328cc Excelsior twin-cylinder 18bhp engine was fitted. The bodywork was made in glassfibre by the coachbuilders, James Whitson & Co, which also made and assembled most of the rest of the car. The Coronet's chassis employed suspension and steering components from the Standard 8.

When it appeared in 1957, it was advertised as "the world's best three-wheeler". It was capable of a top speed of 57mph and did at least offer big car looks. It appears that the Coronet left production in October 1958 with around 250 examples made.

NOBEL

Like the Isetta and Heinkel, the Fuldamobil was another German microcar which found its way into production in many countries worldwide, probably more than any other micro.

It also came to Britain thanks to York-Nobel Industries whose proprietor, Cyril Lord, gave financial weight to the project. With a touch of razamatazz, Soraya (the ex-Shah of Persia) was hired as the

Above: Egg-shaped Nobel 200 was a British-made version of the German Fuldamobil. Its construction was glassfibre and plywood. Below: Who would have thought that the future manufacturer of the world's hairiest car, the AC Cobra, could have produced the Petite microcar from 1953 to 1957.

director of the works. Manufacture was sub-contracted out with the chassis made by the aircraft firm Shorts, the GRP body made by the Bristol Aircraft Company and the whole thing put together in Newtownards, Northern Ireland, by shipbuilders Harland & Wolfe.

The model built in Britain was the Fuldamobil S-7, as introduced in Germany in 1958 and in Britain from February 1959. The British version did differ in one important respect: the German car had four wheels whereas the Nobel 200 was also, and more commonly, available with only three.

In other respects, it was essentially a Fuldamobil: a 191cc Fichtel & Sachs single-cylinder engine, and GRP-and-plywood bodywork atop a steel tube chassis. Cars could be bought either fully-built or in kit form.

Ambitious – some may say unhinged – plans included a production rate of no less than 400 cars a *week* but it quickly became obvious that demand for the Nobel was nowhere near that sort of figure. There were even reports that a batch of Nobels were buried under the A12 in Essex and there were certainly still Nobels in dealers' showrooms two years after the demise of the project in 1962. Moves to merge York-Nobel with Lea-Francis, itself in the process of winding up, sealed the Nobel's fate. In all, about 1000 Nobels were made.

AC

AC Cars is one of the longest-established of all British car firms, yet has almost consistently remained in a penumbra. Its first forays from 1908 concerned the lightweight three-wheeled Auto Carrier Sociable (see

Chapter One). AC made more of a name for itself with the large sports cars and grand tourers it produced after World War Two, including the legendary Cobra.

But AC never lost its microcar roots. It was always involved with the production of invalid carriages and , in the 1950s, it met the needs of the day with the AC Petite, which was an earnest attempt to make a comfortable economy car with three wheels.

It arrived in 1952, although production did not start until 1953. The Petite was a squarish two-to-three-seater with a steel and aluminium body which, from a distance, looked like it should have four wheels. Closer inspection revealed that under the front lay a single wheel which steered the car. The engine, a single-cylinder 346cc Villiers industrial unit, sat in the back. A 50mph (80km/h) top speed was claimed.

The MkII version arrived in 1955, incorporating a slightly larger (353cc) Villiers engine. Whereas the MkI had a smaller front wheel than those at the rear, the Mk2 had the same size wheels all round.

Compared to other microcars, the AC Petite was comfortable and civilised. But it was hardly pretty, charismatic or, for that matter, much of a driving

AC 'PETITE'

60 - 70 MILES PER GALLON
CRUISE AT 33 M.P.H. MAXIMUM 40 M.P.H.
SEAT TWO ADULTS PLUS LUGGAGE
INDEPENDENT SUSPENSION ALL 3 WHEELS
346cc REAR MOUNTED ENGINE
STEERING COLUMN GEAR CHANGE
PANELLED IN ALUMINIUM
TYRES 18" × 3·25" AND 8" × 4"
OVERALL SIZE 10'3" × 4'7" × 4'5"

PRICE EX WORKS £255 PLUS £53. 13. 9 P.T.

experience. AC stated that production was to be "temporarily" suspended in October 1957, but it never restarted. Around 4000 cars were built.

AC went on to become the leading manufacturer of invalid carriages in the UK, producing tens of thousands of the execrable and dangerous devices before the government banned their manufacture in the late 1970s.

MATHIS

Frenchman Emile Mathis was one of the pioneers of aerodynamic design in the 1930s and his first project following the war was a wind-cheating three-wheeler which he dubbed the Mathis VL 333. This stood for Voiture Legere followed by the trinity of fuel consumption (3 litres per 100km – or 94mpg), 3 seats and 3 wheels.

Mathis certainly succeeded as far as aerodynamics was concerned: the 333 had a Cd of just 0.22, thanks to the design input of an engineer called Andreau. The front of the car (where the 707cc engine sat) was very wide at 68.5ins (174cm) and incorporated faired-in lights and grilles.

Above: AC's other three-wheelers were of course invalid carriages, which it built up to the late 1970s. Here, AC director Harry Sidney tries out a 1949 AC aluminium prototype. Below: Elegant Mathis VL333 was an aerodynamic masterpiece, far advanced for its day (1946). Production sadly never began.

With its aluminium bodywork, the Mathis weighed only 970lbs (440kg), which gave it its strength as an economy car. It was displayed at the 1946 Paris Salon and several prototypes were made but, sadly, a production run for this advanced car never

Top: Canoe-like body of the Czech-made Velorex really was made of canvas. Jawa motorbike engines provided the power. Above: Bizarre Teilhol Citadine was a 'gull-nosed' 1970s equivalent of the old bubble cars. It was battery-powered and proved quite popular in urban areas of France.

materialised. Mathis went on to create a larger vehicle with the name 666. He died in 1956.

VELOREX

Three-wheelers have found a foothold in most countries of the world at one time or another. In Czechoslovakia, a three-wheeler became one of the longest-surviving trikes of all: the Velorex, made in Rychnov, lasted from 1954 right up until 1971.

Perhaps the strangest facet of the Velorex was its canoe-like construction. Over a steel tube space frame, canvas panels were stretched and then fastened. The front and rear panels had stud fixings so that owners could remove them. A De Luxe version with all-steel panels was offered for those with misgivings about canvas bodywork.

Velorex also made motorbikes and took its

engines from the Jawa range: 250cc single-cylinder and 350cc two-cylinder two-strokes were used to drive the single rear wheel. A four-wheeled model also made a late appearance but did not enter production.

TEILHOL

Teilhol is a well-known name in France as the constructor, since 1970, of the Rodeo 'jeeps' for Renault. It branched out in 1972 with the construction of its own electric car, the Citadine.

To seasoned eyes, this might have been seen as the return of the Isetta. The shape was more angular but the profile was distinctively bubble car-like. There was even a front-opening door, albeit hinged at the top. A hatchback allowed entry to a rear parcel area.

The Citadine used a GRP body on top of a tubular chassis. Propulsion came from a 48 volt electric motor driving the single rear wheel. A top speed of 31mph (50km/h) was quoted and the range could be as high as 60 miles (100km). Despite its tiny size (only 7ft or 212cm long), the weight of the batteries made it very heavy: all of half a ton (500kg). An electric three-wheeled 'pick-up' version was called the Citacom.

Teilhol's electric three-wheelers remained available until the mid-1980s, by which time its petrochemical-burning four-wheeled micro partners had taken over the production lines.

Ugly as sin, the CEDRE poses incongruously at the Palais de Versailles. It was bought mainly by Parisians.

CEDRE

Little more than a shed on three wheels with a sliding perspex door, the CEDRE was historic in that it was one of the first of the new breed of French micro three-wheelers and also the last to leave production.

The brainchild of Toulouse-based engineer Francois Guerbet, the CEDRE was unusual in being offered only with electric power. Its 1200 watt motor could take it about 35 miles at a top speed of just 30mph. This single-seater was absolutely the most basic type of transportation. Style it did not have, in empty bucket loads; comfort – hah, I blow raspberries at your comfort; speed – zat is but a hamster, monsieur.

Apart from an extremely eccentric five-wheeled version, with four wheels set at the back, Guerbet always stuck to the three-wheeled format. At least he did until no-one wanted his cars any more, which occurred in around 1987.

VITREX

In its short life, Vitrex Industries of Paris was a prolific developer of microcars. It began its activities in 1974 with the Riboud, a very basic micro designed by an architect called Jacques Riboud and created by a French buggy manufacturer, Marland.

The Riboud used a 47cc 2.4bhp Sachs engine in a rather plain two-seater open body. Unusually, it was offered in both three- and four-wheeled forms. It filled a need, though, and was the cheapest *voiturette* around at 6430F (in 1979). And it sold well: 560 in 1974 and 530 the following year.

Also in 1974 came the Addax. This was actually made by a different firm (ECAM) in Chambly and was even more spartan than the Riboud. A three-wheeled two-seater, the Addax used either a 47cc or 50cc engine with an automatic and three-speed manual gearbox respectively. There were also *Bord de Mer* and even *Sport* versions!

Vitrex's activities ceased just into the 1980s. Its three-wheelers were simply too crude for the developing tastes of French rural OAPs.

AROLA

One of the most successful of all French microcars was the Arola. It virtually created the form of future *voiturettes*.

Cuddly Arola was a trail-blazer in the French microcar world. Its format of utter simplicity, tiny moped engine and cheap price led it to sell in its thousands.

First presented in January 1976, the Arola from Lyon was the brainchild of Daniel Manon. It was a very simple polyester-and-glassfibre-bodied design with three wheels. Its single-cylinder air-cooled two-stroke Sachs engine of just 47cc capacity was typical of the genre. Producing only 3bhp, it was not even powerful enough to propel the 242lb (110kg) car to the permitted top speed of 45km/h (27mph) – it puffed its last at 25mph!

Still, it looked quite cute and had funky transparent plastic doors. It was also damn' cheap, at 7880 Francs in 1978, and was soon selling no less than 350 examples a month. In 1978, a version with a pick-up tray tacked on the back was launched under the name Super Pratique (or SP).

A four-wheeled version with a Motobecane 50cc engine soon followed, and that really sounded the death-knell for the wee tripeds, which were withdrawn just into the 1980s, but by 1983 the firm had in any case ceased its activities.

ACOMA

This Angers-based enterprise was one of the early French microcar makers. It typified in many ways the crudity of those early years, yet proved how little you had to do to sell a lot of cars.

Born as early as 1975, Acoma quickly took 30% of the French microcar market, selling 3000 cars a year by 1982. Its success was based on the Mini-Comtesse, a typically idiosyncratic looking single-seat thing with polyester bodywork. It had a single front wheel and an odd folding gullwing door. Placing the 50cc Motobecane engine in the front of the car, where the single wheel sat, obviously did not help its cornering abilities. The magazine *L'Auto-Journal* tested one in 1976 and concluded that it was so unstable the authorities ought to do something about it!

They didn't – but Acoma did. In 1978, they made the Mini-Comtesse into a four-wheeler and another dreadful three-wheeler bit the dust.

ALL CARS

The little Charly was first presented by a firm called Autozodiaco in November 1974. An amusing and genially shaped three-wheeler, it used a plastic two-seater body composed entirely of straight lines. Typical of Italian city cars, it used a Minarelli 49cc engine.

All-Cars Snuggy rates as one of the all-time great names of the motoring world. This Italian tricycle was even half stylish.

Production had transferred to a new enterprise called All Cars by 1978. The model now used a 50cc Morini 4.5bhp engine and was renamed, brilliantly, the Snuggy. A new convertible version (painted in obligatory khaki with a spare wheel on the back) was also introduced with the yet more inspired name of Snuggy Tobrouk. Later versions switched again to Motobecane 50cc engines and were even offered with, by its standards, pretty darn rorty 250cc units.

The design was so good that the Italian microcar grand-daddy, Lawil, made a more or less direct copy of it. But by 1985, All Cars had met its Tobrouk and the name disappeared.

BMA

Symmetrical shapes which minimise tooling costs are not uncommon: the Champion and Dornier Delta of the 1950s are but two examples. However, there was no car quite as bizarrely symmetrical as the BMA Brio.

This was quite the most surreal microcar offering from Italy, a country noted for its outlandish *carrozzerie*. Its polyester resin bodywork resembled a wedge of sculptured gorgonzola turned on its edge. The fully convertible version was hardly more normal.

Technically, the Brio recalled the days of cyclecars and the absolute minimum in transportation. Its tiny 47cc Sachs engine sat in the tail, from where it drove the rear right wheel only. This putt-putted the Brio to a distinctly un-brio-like top speed of just 23mph (37km/h).

It had joined, in 1978, one of the more established Italian microcars, the BMA Amica, first seen in 1971. This was another three-wheeler, rather larger than the Brio, which sported engines from 50cc up to 223cc. Its plastic bodywork featured gullwing doors, no less.

BMA introduced its Nuova Amica in 1980. This had rather more normal-looking bodywork and three or four wheels, offered with a choice of 50cc, 125cc or 250cc petrol engines and a 360cc diesel.

BMA products were marketed in France throughout the 1970s and into the 1980s, which helped BMA sell around 500 cars per year. The Brio vanished in about 1986, leaving only the two Amica models to continue the line. They remain available at the time of writing, with 125cc or 250cc engine options.

BAMBY

A microcar enthusiast, Hull-based Alan Evans was inspired by his acquisition of a Peel P50 (see above) to attempt to create a modern equivalent. In 1983 his Bamby made its bow.

Above: As unhinged as they get: drugs must have played their part in the styling of the Italian BMA Brio. A cabriolet version was also made. Below: Inspired by the Peel P50, Hull man Alan Evans built the Bamby in 1983 as a modern version – and it actually went on sale, albeit for only a year.

Like the Peel, the original Bamby was a single-seater glassfibre-bodied three-wheeler with a 49cc engine. It weighed all of 235lbs (107kg) and could return 100mpg. And it looked pretty good, too, although its price of £1,597 was decidedly on the high side.

Soon some design changes were made: the single gullwing door was changed to a conventionally hinged door, there were twin headlamps in place of the original cyclops lamp and the air vents, which had let a wasp into one customer's car, were blocked off using a kitchen sieve. The engine was progressively upgraded from a 49cc Minarelli to Yamaha, then Suzuki moped units.

An initial production rate of 20 per month proved over-optimistic and the Bamby died after only a year or so, as founder Alan Evans left the project in the hands of a

Words can hardly describe the charms of the Cursor, which was touted as a 'GT hatchback convertible'. It had a 50cc moped engine!

businessman who liquidated the venture within a matter of months. Probably around 50 Bambys had been made in total.

CURSOR

Alan Hatswell's Replicar Ltd, purveyors of kit-form replicas of Bugattis, Jaguars and Ferraris, launched its 'revolutionary micro vehicle' in 1985. And a decidedly strange beast it was.

Called the Cursor, it was a single-seat three-wheeler whose main selling-point was that it was classed as a moped and could therefore be driven by 16 year-olds. Its extremely odd glassfibre body sat on top of a tubular steel chassis and the whole thing looked more like an escapee from the fairground than something in which to burble down the dual carriageways.

Cryptically described as a "GT hatchback convertible", the Cursor boasted nothing more sporting than a 49cc Suzuki CS50 moped engine; presumably the GT tag derived from the fact that it was mid-mounted. A top speed of 30mph was offset by a fuel consumption of about 90mpg, and all for £1,724.

After about 50 had been made, a two-seater version followed with a more powerful Suzuki CP50 engine and gullwing doors fitted. The final ten or so of the 50 two-seaters built had Honda Vision moped engines. Most of the later models were exported to Vienna, Austria.

Replicar claimed grandly of the Cursor that: "The impact on driving will be much the same as when the Mini was launched in the late 1950s". In fact, drivers (even of the 16 year-old variety) hardly gave it a cursory glance. Its chances cannot have been helped by the appearance at the London Motorfair of a Cursor adorned in gold metalflake paint! The project was sold on to a firm in Belgium, where its production existence remains in question at the time of writing.

Chapter 4

The Plastic Pig: The Reliant

Is there any three-wheeler more celebrated than the Reliant? From the early days of motoring, Reliant has been there, consistently supplying three-wheeled carriages to an insatiable British market. When all others abandoned the three-wheeled format, Reliant soldiered on. And even today, long after most people think that the three-wheeler (and even the Reliant) is dead and gone, you can still buy a brand new Reliant trike.

The success of the Reliant is entirely due to the peculiar law of the land which allows three-wheelers to be driven on a motorbike licence. If it were not for this law, the Reliant would surely be long since dead and buried. As it is, a healthy band of (usually older) customers continues to buy the Reliant. Almost inevitably, they have always done so and will probably never change. However, a bizarre and frankly mystifying statistic is that one in four buyers of new Rialtos holds a car driving licence and need not buy a three-wheeler.

The origins of Reliant go back to Raleigh, the famous Nottingham maker of bicycles. As early as 1905, it had tried its hand at car manufacture, but it was not until 1933 that the first true production Raleigh motor car hit the streets, and it was a three-wheeler. To liberate the maximum amount of space for four passengers, Raleigh adopted a single front wheel approach – a format long since abandoned in Britain in favour of the Morgan-style configuration. So it set the tone for the legend which would become... Reliant!

The Raleigh Safety Seven was a very basic machine designed by Mr T.L. Williams as a light delivery wagon. It had a single front wheel mounted

Delightful rendering of the 1933 Raleigh Safety Seven saloon – the forerunner of the Reliant. Were people really that small in the 1930s?

on motorcycle-type forks, with a 742cc V-twin engine sited behind it driving the rear wheels by shaft through a three-speed gearbox. In its saloon car version, four seats were provided within the open metal bodywork. The cost was £110 5s.

However, Raleigh decided to put and end to its engine-powered products, so in 1934 Williams set to work developing the idea for production on his own. The following year, he set up Reliant Engineering at an old bus garage in Tamworth, Staffordshire – the place where all Reliants would be made in future – and began manufacture of the Reliant three-wheeler in 7cwt van form only.

The engine was a single-cylinder air-cooled 600cc JAP unit, again driving the rear wheels by chain through a three-speed gearbox with reverse. In 1936, a 10cwt twin-cylinder JAP model with shaft drive joined the 7cwt version. By this time, Reliant was building its own bodies. In 1937, Reliant began fitting Austin

Above: The first in a long line: the 1951 Reliant Regal. Bodywork was aluminium over ash and the engine derived from the pre-war Austin Seven. Below: The MkII Regal had a new grille and rounded windscreen corners.

Seven 747cc engines in its vans (8cwt and 12cwt).

The production process got even more adventurous in 1939, when the momentous step was taken to power the Reliant van with its own development of the Austin Seven engine, as Austin's production was coming to an end.

Production of the so-called girder fork vans continued after World War II, latterly dubbed the Regent and Prince Regent. These vans continued in production until 1955, when they were replaced by the new Regal van. The Regal saloon had already been launched in 1951 as Reliant's first passenger three-wheeler.

RELIANT REGAL MKI-VI

The Reliant Regal was first shown at the Cycle and Motor Show in November 1951, although production did not actually begin until January 1953. It followed the basic mechanical layout of the old van, complete with its 747cc 16bhp four-cylinder engine, derived from the Austin Seven's. The box section pressed steel chassis was fitted with torsion bar springing for the front wheel (on a long stub axle) and semi-elliptic springs for the live rear axle. Braking was hydraulic, and the four-speed gearbox also incorporated a reverse gear – sophisticated stuff!

The new car-like bodywork was in aluminium alloy over an ash frame and could seat four people, and was initially available in open form only. It was definitely a cut above the other economy three-wheelers of the day, like the Bond and Gordon, and carried a commensurate price tag of £352. It was also more substantial than any other three-wheeler, attempting to offer the accommodation and

performance of a larger car. It weighed under 8cwt, allowing it a top speed of approaching 60mph and fuel consumption around 55mpg.

Driving it was probably a lot better than most of the three-wheelers of the 1950s, but it wasn't any great shakes compared to, say, an Austin Seven. The handling with the weight of the engine over the front wheel was distinctly iffy and the ride was extremely poor. Although interior space was good by three-wheeler standards, it was somewhat compromised by the bulge created in the cabin behind which sat the engine. The problem was that the engine and gearbox assembly had to be sited rather far back in the chassis to clear the central front wheel, and Reliant owners quickly became used to the 'coal scuttle' effect, with a sizeable bulge intruding between the passengers' legs.

In May 1954 came the Regal MkII, identifiable by its new front grille and rounded windscreen corners. A Hardtop model was offered from November 1955, with a glassfibre roof coloured in a contrasting hue.

Glassfibre gradually became more prevalent in the Regal, with the engine cover and rear panels being moulded from the new material from early 1956 and, with the MkIII of November 1956, the entire body moulded from plastic (although still with wooden strengthening beams).

The MkIII's body style was all-new, longer and wider, with far more rounded lines. The doors were wider and the waistline was higher, although there were still sidescreens instead of windows. You even got flashing indicators as standard! There were open Coupe and enclosed Hardtop versions as before.

For all the revolution in the bodywork department, the mechanical side of things remained almost

completely unchanged apart from synchromesh on the upper three gears. The same 6ft 2in wheelbase chassis remained, as did the suspension, brakes and engine. The latter was given a redesigned camshaft in 1957 for improved power output.

In September 1958 came the Regal MkIV, again in Coupe and Hardtop styles. Some of the changes advertised for it appear to have been fitted on late MkIII models, probably from around April 1958. Principally this consisted of an improved chassis, allowing the engine to be sited further forward. The engine/gearbox assembly still protruded severely into the passenger compartment, but not by quite as much. The front suspension was now by Armstrong damper and the wheel size was reduced from 14in to 13in. Finally, 12 volt electrics and vertically sliding windows were adopted.

The model only lasted a matter of months before the MkV replaced it in May 1959. This brought a new body style (saloon form only) on a fractionally longer wheelbase, said to offer more interior space. At last you got an opening boot and such luxuries as twin windscreen wipers and safety glass all round.

The final development of the original-type Regal was the MkVI of autumn 1960, by which time Reliant was easily the largest manufacturer of three-wheelers in Britain. Mechanically the MkVI was identical to its predecessor, but the bodywork was altered to provide more rear headroom and a slight overhang. The dashboard was redesigned with a single central dial.

RELIANT REGAL 3/25 and 3/30

In October 1962 came the brand new Reliant Regal, dubbed the Regal 3/25 because it had three wheels and 25bhp. At last there was a major update in styling in the form of a sharp and angular treatment, very reminiscent of the Ford Anglia, only uglier. Bodywork remained all-glassfibre and initially in saloon form only, but there was considerably more interior space than in the old Regal.

The biggest change was the adoption of Reliant's own diecast all-alloy engine, developed from the old Austin Seven unit. This 598cc four-cylinder OHV unit developed 25bhp at 5250rpm and was the very first all-aluminium engine built in series in Britain.

Weight remained at under the legal limit of 8cwt, so performance was much better: up to 65mph was possible. The mechanical side of the Regal was very much as before, with the same perimeter frame chassis and the same gearbox.

Reliant soon branched out into four-wheelers with the sporting Sabre and a new economy model, the Rebel, but its main business remained three-wheelers.

By 1968, it had sold some 50,000 of the new Regal and was making up to 20,000 cars a year – ranking it as the second-largest British-owned firm after BLMC.

In late 1967 came the 3/30, which was basically the same car with an expanded 701cc version of the all-aluminium engine, developing 30bhp. There were now

Left: Glamorous shot of the all-new 1962 Regal 3/25. If there was one thing the Regal was not, *it was a bird-puller. Top: Breezeway-style rear window did nothing for the looks of the Regal 3/25. Still, it became by far the best-selling three-wheeler ever. Bottom: New front end and a larger and more powerful engine for the Regal 3/30 launched in 1967.*

Reliant Robin, which has always been a lone triped in a world of quadrupeds. Thanks to Jasper Carrott and others, it became the butt of a thousand jokes, such as *'What do you call a Reliant Robin with a football inside it? A whistle'*. The police coined the phrase 'plastic pigs' to describe them, and the name stuck.

The all-new Reliant Robin arrived in October 1973. In layout, it followed the style of the Regal, with a new twin-rail chassis in which was slung the familiar alloy four-pot engine – but now bored out to 748cc with 32bhp on tap for a maximum speed of 73mph. Economy remained a strong marketing feature, with an average of around 45mpg.

For 1973, the new Robin looked very modern with its neat, Tom Karen-penned lines. It even had a hatchback of sorts, a hinging glass door at the back which allowed access to a much more generous boot

Top: The infamous Reliant Robin, the butt of Jasper Carrott's wit and pet hate of HM's police force. Note the racy optional alloy wheels. Right: This is a rare Jubilee special edition of the Robin. Bottom right: Alongside the Rialto, the Robin name was revived for the new hatchback version of the Reliant in 1989. The nostalgia must have welled up among Reliant's ex-biker clientele.

estate and van versions and, amazingly, a GT version offered by a Reliant dealer called Two Strokes of Stanmore. This had a tweaked 31bhp engine which the firm claimed gave it "quite startling" performance...

Reliant's Regal lasted until 1973, when it was replaced by the Robin. At that stage, the Regal was probably the best-selling three-wheeler ever made, with an annual production total of about 12,000 – a figure which has never been repeated in Reliant's history.

RELIANT ROBIN

In 1969, Reliant bought out its only rival, Bond, and quickly ceased production of the 875. That meant that, for the first time in history, Reliant had the three-wheeler market all to itself. As demand remained quite buoyant throughout the ensuing years, this was an extremely healthy state of affairs for the Tamworth firm. Three-wheelers remained Reliant's staple offering, even with the Scimitar GTE grand tourer in regular production. But the market was at its peak in 1972 (when 13,000 Regals were sold), after which it slowly began to decline.

Reliant had also cultivated a good working liaison with Tom Karen of Ogle Design, the first fruit of which was the Scimitar sports car. Also from Karen's pen came the whacky Bond Bug (see Chapter Five). The Bug used a version of the forthcoming Robin chassis, which was thicker yet lighter than the Regal's.

There can hardly be a more infamous car than the

Above: The Pride of Peckham: Del Trotter's 'luvly motor' in the TV series Only Fools and Horses *was a Regal van. It can now be seen in the Cars of the Stars museum in Keswick, Cumbria. Below: January 1995: new Reliant MD Peter Hall (left) beside the rescued Robin.*

with a folding rear bench seat. If you were desperate for more luggage space, you could order an estate or van version with a large side-hinging rear door and extended rear bodywork. The body of both models was, naturally, all-glassfibre, with some detailing using the new injection-moulding process.

A new all-syncromesh gearbox was used and a cable-operated clutch appeared on a Reliant three-wheeler for the first time. The front suspension remained basically the same as the old Regal, but at the rear you now got single-leaf semi-elliptic springs instead of multi-leafs, plus an anti-roll bar. Meanwhile, the wheels had shrunk to Mini-sized 10-inchers.

The interior of the Robin was much more comfortable, with a proper dash and centre console and fresh-air ventilation. For some £48 more than the basic Robin (which cost £801), you could buy a Super Robin with superior trim and equipment. Go for the optional alloy wheels and you could even make it look quite sporty...

The Robin was joined by the four-wheeled Kitten in 1975, at which time the Robin got an expanded 848cc engine with no less than 40bhp on tap. The Robin bumbled along, selling reasonably well, until it was replaced by the Rialto in 1981.

RELIANT RIALTO

The Rialto, which arrived at the Earls Court Motor Show in October 1981, was little more than a warmed-over Robin. It looked a little different, with its sloping nose and sculptured GRP bumpers, but it couldn't hide the fact that it was really just a dressed-up Robin. It reverted to single-leaf rear suspension, where late Robins had gained double-leafers, but it now had a galvanised chassis and interior engine access covers, *a la* Regal. The gear lever was also now canted over towards the driver. Amazingly, cross-ply tyres were still standard; if you wanted radials, that cost extra.

The old 'saloon' body style was deleted: only the estate-type body with the side-hinging door was now available. The most basic Rialto was the van (cost £2924), followed by the standard model (£3424), up to the GLS (£3724) which boasted cloth trim, carpeted boot and spare wheel cover. Rialtos continued to find homes with ex-bikers, but a significant one in four Rialto buyers did possess car driving licences. So why did they buy three-wheelers? No satisfactory explanation has ever been given to this motoring mystery.

Reliant did a Land's End to John o' Groats run in a Rialto, which went to prove how economical the car remained: at an average speed of 54.1mph, the wee piglet returned no less than 60.1mpg.

The Rialto 2 arrived in 1984, with minor improvements to its specification. More significant was the revival in August 1989 of the Robin name. This was as a slightly more up-market version of the Rialto with, at last, a 'proper' hatchback tailgate hinging along its top edge. You also got new rear end treatment: a different shape, new bumper and larger rear light clusters.

Surprisingly, the Robin/Rialto's appeal was not

confined to Britain. Large numbers were exported to the Netherlands and to Austria. Other countries were keen to build the Rialto in their homelands: Syria, Uganda, Pakistan and Russia all applied to acquire the right to make the three-wheeler.

The current Reliant range: Robin hatchback, Rialto van and Rialto estate.

An unforgettable piece of motoring folklore was the incident where a Robin was stopped by the police for doing 104mph on the M20. This was a spur for *The Sun* to launch a 'Del Boy Derby' (a yellow Reliant Regal van was the unlikely co-star of BBC TV's comedy series *Only Fools and Horses*). One brave owner turned up to the Goodwood race in a V8 powered Robin.

In October 1990, Reliant went bankrupt. Part of the problem was the disappointing sales of its Scimitar SS1 sports cars, in which so much had been invested. But the main reason was the investment of the major shareholders in the property market. When that particular balloon burst in the late 1980s, Reliant sunk with it.

The Reliant three-wheeler looked like it might finally have reached the end of the line. But in contrast to the Scimitar, the Rialto had a healthy order book: no less than 233 were on order when the receivers stepped in. This was enough to persuade Beans Engineering, the firm which had been building the engines and gearboxes for the Rialto, to try and recover its losses. It bought up the rights to Reliant in August 1991 and put the Rialto and Robin back into production at the rate of 32 per week.

Interestingly, during the break in production prices of used Rialtos had soared due to the shortfall in supply. Reliant dealers probably made more money selling old Rialtos than they had ever done with new ones!

The Rialto/Robin was an economy car, but its price was not cheap. In 1994, the entry price for a Rialto was £6076 – some £380 more than a Mini – and a Robin cost £6333. However, price was never a problem for Reliant, since most of its (typically elderly) customers had plenty of spare cash saved up. There were even instances where new Reliants were bought new with £10 notes stuffed into a tin.

By late 1994, Reliant was again in trouble. Parent company Beans Engineering suffered bad debts resulting from its other engineering work, and Reliant was sucked under as Beans went bankrupt

and the receivers moved in for a second time in just over four years. However, as Reliant was obviously a viable concern, a buyer was quickly found in the form of the Avonex Group, a motor and aviation parts supplier.

Three-wheeler production in fact continued uninterrupted and at the time of writing its future looks more secure, since Avonex has declared its intention to develop its newly acquired models. It also stated that further export markets would be opened up. Certainly the demand for Reliant trikes is as healthy now as it has been for the last ten years – and the Reliant remains firmly on the motoring map.

MISCELLANEOUS RELIANT NUGGETS

Reliant also produced a three-wheeled commercial vehicle called the Ant. The rights to the Ant were bought by coachbuilders Hooper in the 1980s. Until recently, the tooling had been in the hands of classic car restorers Hutson, but in 1995 the Ant returned to the roost when Reliant bought it back. Also of interest is the fact that a Robin was modified by an American firm known as Zoe, which offered the model with huge extended rear wheel arches and a choice of hybrid or electric power.

RELIANT'S RIVAL: THE BOND 875

In 1966, production of the archaic Bond Minicar had finally come to an end (see Chapter Three). In its place, a new three-wheeler was launched – but this was an entirely different pot of potatoes from the old

Top: The Reliant Ant became a familiar sight on British roads. The rear bodywork could be tailored to your requirements. Above: Imp-engined Bond 875 was reportedly terrifying to drive. It was the only serious rival to Reliant during the 1960s, but it never sold in anything like the same numbers. Right: The MkII version was publicized with this scarcely credible advertising line. The biggest change was a new front end.

Minicar, and took Bond firmly into the market territory occupied by Reliant.

The new Bond 875 took its name from the cylinder capacity of the engine it used – the Hillman Imp's. As per the Imp, this was located at the rear of the body, between the two rear wheels, which made a lot more sense as far as stability and roadholding were concerned.

Although the Bond used the detuned commercial version of the 875cc engine (it developed 34bhp instead of 39bhp), it still represented a mighty wodge of power for a car with only one front wheel. A top speed of 82mph was possible, with 0-60mph coming up in 17.4sec – truly scorching performance by three-

wheeler standards of the day. Despite the better weight distribution, the 875 acquired a reputation for being a bit of a handful around corners. Owners became accustomed to watching their own rear ends waltz past them on tight bends.

The 875 had an enclosed four-seater glassfibre body which was also rather more accommodating than the old-style Bonds. A Ranger Van version was also available, and a prototype estate was made but did not enter production. The Mk2 version of the saloon in 1967 had a redesigned front end with rectangular headlamps, but the model died when arch-rivals Reliant bought up the company in 1969 and then closed down the old Bond factory in Preston the following year.

With that, the 875 died – the last of the 'true' Bonds. A grand total of 3431 Bond 875s had been built, which was a lot by Bond standards but a drop in the ocean compared to Reliant. Reliant went on to use the Bond name on a new fun car which it launched in 1970: the zany, far-out, spaced-out Bond Bug. For that story, you'll have to step boldly into the decade of patch pockets, platforms and Emerson, Lake & Palmer... the 1970s. Go to Chapter Five. Do not pass Go. Do not collect £200.

Chapter 5

Three for Fun: 1970s Fun Cars

Apart from the Reliant, at the dawn of the 1970s there were virtually no three-wheelers left on the British market. The mass-produced trike and micro-trike were a thing of the past.

But in the wake of a great boom in so-called 'fun cars' in the early 1970s, there arrived a small but rich vein of unusual fun trikes, usually sold in kit form for assembly by the customer. These were typically outlandish, pandering to the daze of psychedelia induced by tripped-out beach buggies. As far as most such customers were concerned, having only three wheels was a bonus: it was just a little bit more 'far out' than your average dayglo-purple dune machine.

Just like buggies, however, the novelty quickly wore off. In Britain, at least, three-wheelers and fun

did not go together, and virtually all of them were gone by the end of the decade – only to return in rather a different form in the great kit car boom of the 1980s (see Chapter Seven).

BOND BUG

No car typified the heady swoon of the early 1970s more than the Bond Bug. Nothing like it had ever been seen before and, perhaps unsurprisingly, nothing like it

Spaceship Bug: In 1970, the tiny Bond Bug drew more looks than a Lamborghini Miura. Obligatory orange paint, decal mania and frogeye headlamps may have helped.

Less equipment and a low-compression engine with 2bhp less featured on the cheaper Bond Bug 700E.

has ever appeared since.

The Bug was born as an idea in Czech-born designer Tom Karen's head. Karen was the head of the slightly eccentric British design company Ogle Design and had long wanted to do a completely original 'fun' three-wheeler on a Reliant chassis. Karen had worked with Reliant since 1963 and had frequently suggested such a machine to the Tamworth car maker. When Reliant bought Bond in 1969, ceasing production of the Bond 875, Karen finally got his chance. He persuaded them to relaunch the Bond marque with a whacky three-wheeler of his own devising.

The Bond Bug was a bold design presented as a car for those too young to be square. It cleverly combined the economies of three-wheeled motoring with a sporting, youthful image. Using a modified and shortened version of the forthcoming Reliant Robin chassis as its basis, the rest of the mechanical package came from the then current Reliant Regal.

Its most striking feature was a one-piece canopy which tilted forward on a gas strut to allow entry; removable sidescreens provided ventilation and there was a rudimentary heater. There were only two seats, simply cushions placed over moulded-in hollows, and a small amount of luggage space found by opening a wooden bootlid in the sharply cut-off tail. The passengers sat in a reclined position with the engine sitting between their knees. To get at the engine, a cover had to be taken off from within the cockpit:

probably the only car where changing the plugs requires you to keep the door open!

The wedge shaped body was available in any colour you liked – as long as it was bright tangerine! The use of aircraft-type black decals, indicating the required octane level of the fuel and instructions for opening the canopy, was a revolutionary touch of which Karen was proud.

The Bug was publically launched in June 1970 as 'The fun car of the seventies'. At the press launch party in May 1970 at Woburn Abbey, one over-enthusiastic journalist called Stuart Marshall managed to roll a Bug right over, which set the tone for future encounters with owners. Handling was not as bad as it might have been thanks to four rear trailing arms, an anti-roll bar and a Panhard rod, but a single front wheel with a lot of weight over it is a sure recipe for tumbles. As the crashes rolled in, the Bug's insurance grouping leapt up...

Initially it was intended to sell the Bug in three versions: the 700, 700E and 700ES. In the event the base 700 never entered production: only one prototype was ever built. The entry-level 700E used the 29bhp engine, while the popular ES used the high compression (31bhp) version of the 701cc Regal/Rebel engine, sufficient to power it to a top speed of 77mph. In addition, the ES came with better trim, rim embellishers and – the luxury of it! – a spare wheel. The price was a rather steep £579 for the E and £629 for the ES.

Lots of magazines got their hands on Bugs for road testing, and most were pretty complimentary. Autocar even predicted that it would become "the Ford Mustang of its class", hinting that it would sell very well and come to be regarded as 'the car to own'. Sadly, that didn't happen. Perhaps it was the price – the ES cost more than a Hillman Imp or Mini – perhaps it was the sheer impracticality of a car with only two seats and virtually no luggage space. Whatever the reason, the Bug never did quite catch.

Early Bugs were built at Bond's old Preston factory, but following Reliant's decision to close the works in 1970, production transferred to Tamworth. At that stage, about 350 had been made.

From October 1973, Bugs received the bigger 748cc engine and the models became known as the

750E and 750ES. Faced with dramatically declining sales for a car which had always cost Reliant a lot to make, production came to a close in May 1974 as Reliant concentrated on production of the new Robin. Around 2270 Bugs had been made. It took a long time to sell the existing stock, the very last cars being registered in 1975. Not only was that the end of the Bug, it was the end of the Bond name after some 25 years.

BUG FOLLOW-UPS

SP Spi-Tri: There were a couple of curious addenda to the Bug story in the form of two revivals. The first was an American version of the car. A firm called Structural Plastic Inc of Tulsa, Oklahoma, developed an electrically-powered prototype during the 1980s called the SP Spi-Tri using a Bug shell extended by several inches between the cockpit and rear wheel. It claimed a top speed of 50mph and a range of 40 miles.

Later versions of the Spi-Tri, which it is believed did enter production, had enormous impact bumpers and larger diameter wheels.

WMC Bug: Mike Webster, a keen microcar enthusiast and collector, was also a fan of the Bond Bug. He accumulated no less than five examples in various states. In 1990, he and his brother Gary came across some original Bug moulds and managed to make them serviceable. Forming a new firm, the

Top: This elongated Bug is an American Spi-Tri, complete with preposterous impact bumpers. Few were made. Above: Four wheels on my wagon... The Bug relaunched by WMC for the 'nineties could be ordered with the heresy of four wheels, or as a three-wheeler on this modified chassis. Below left: Up she goes! The roof, widscreen and sidescreens all rose as one on a gas strut to allow entry. The upper sidescreens were removable for fresh air motoring.

Webster Motor Company, they relaunched the Bug in Britain as the WMC Bug.

Everyone knows the Bond Bug as a three-wheeler, but Bond did make two four-wheeled prototypes. The first was a bit of a joke: two Bugs joined back-to-back to create a diamond-pattern four-wheeler as a pure show car. The second was a conventional machine.

WMC decided to enter production with a four-wheeler specially modified by themselves. It had 10-inch wheels at the front and 12-inchers at the rear. But there was a large response from potential customers who wanted a three-wheeled kit – to create, in effect, a brand new Bug. There were more Bug fans out there than had been realised! For the three-wheeler model, the Bond name was actually resurrected and the car was officially sold as a Bond Bug.

WMC developed a new but broadly similar ladder chassis designed to accept as many parts as possible from the donor car: the Reliant Robin/Rialto. Hence the engine could be the 748cc unit originally used in the Bug, but more likely the later 41bhp 850cc engine.

Amazing super-performance interpretation of the Bug concept came from the pen of Ogle's Glynn Kerr and dates from 1991. (Glynn Kerr)

With this in place, a top speed of 100mph was claimed!

A new rear suspension was developed with a five-link system incorporating a Panhard rod stretching the full width of the rear track. At the front, standard Robin suspension was employed.

Many parts were reproduced to mimic the Bond, like the seat cushions, single wiper and opening canopy, and you could fit Regal instruments for the authentic look. They were even sold in an approximation of the original tangerine colour (actually a Reliant orange used on the Rialto) and the black graphics could be duplicated. WMC claimed that you would have to be an expert to tell their Bug apart from the original.

However, if you preferred to modernise your Bug, you could do so with circular dials, inertia reel seat belts, laminated windscreen and folding GRP side screens which hinged like doors so that you could get in without having to lift the canopy every time.

There was also now a choice of 10, 12 or 13 inch wheels in place of the Bond's 10 inchers. And there was a curious Sport option which was basically a Bug with a cut-down canopy and aero screens for pure summer use.

One other intriguing facet of Mike Webster's cottage manufacturing operation was his use of a BRM-developed 850cc OHC engine based on the Reliant block. This was claimed to develop no less

than 70bhp! He intended to use this engine in a forthcoming project based on the Bug chassis: no less than a revived, stretched and widened Berkeley – which was a car originally designed by Lawrie Bond. However, this was to be a four-wheeler (although the original Berkeley from 1960 was indeed built as a three-wheeler with its single wheel at the opposite end to the Bug's – see Chapter Three).

WMC's three-wheeled Bug sold in kit form at around the £2000 mark. Even though immaculate original Bond Bugs could be bought for much less than that, WMC have sold about a dozen three-wheeled Bugs to date. The four-wheeled version has so far proven, perhaps understandably, the more popular choice. The company still operates today from Mike Webster's home at Braishfield in Hampshire.

OGLE 21ST ANNIVERSARY BUG

As the 21st birthday of the Bond Bug loomed in 1991, a new design manager was appointed at Ogle in the form of Glynn Kerr. His previous work had included jobs at TVR and BMW and freelance design for various motorbike makers, including Triumph and Yamaha (for whom he designed the TDM850).

Kerr wanted to use the Bug's 21st anniversary as a platform to launch a new design ideal at Ogle. He wanted to bring Ogle back into the car design arena from which it had moved away since the 1970s. So he penned a startling all-new Bug concept.

The 'new' Bug reversed its configuration, with two wheels at the front. In line with Kerr's motorbike background, it was a real cross between 'bike and car. The passengers were seated in open pods, staggered so that the engine could be fitted behind the driver. That engine was intended to be a Yamaha 1200 Zeemax unit, so one can surmise that the new Bug would have been an opposite for the original performance levels, too.

However, the Bug concept never got a chance to germinate. Kerr left Ogle within three months and the design was never given the exposure it deserved. Some of the themes did crop on the later Grinnall Scorpion, however...

Above: A pair of the rare AF Grand Prix built by Alexander Fraser during the 1970s. Left: Like a three-wheeled wardrobe on its side, commented one journalist of the 1971 AF Spider. Despite its resemblance to a boat, sadly it did not float. Below: Unlike the sharp-ended Spider, the Grand Prix had a rounded rump and cycle front wings.

AF SPIDER and GRAND PRIX

Were it not for the zap-pod Bond Bug, the AF series would surely have been the most barmy three-wheeler in existence. Alexander T. Fraser was a fervent Morgan three-wheeler fanatic and the AF was his own interpretation of the idea. In association with Colin Crabbe, he designed and built a small Mini-based trike in 1971 with the name AB1.

The marine ply monocoque body/chassis was mated to a standard Mini front subframe, while a special steel subframe with a single Mini trailing arm supported the pointed tail – although without the Mini's rubber cone, a coil/spring damper doing the work. The tail was in aluminium on the prototype, but later cars had glassfibre tails.

The AB1 didn't look much like a classic Morgan, but it had a vintage flavour with its exposed Mini engine and headlamps sited on the waist-high running boards. Antique Automobiles Ltd of Baston, Peterborough, offered AB1 body/chassis units in 1971 from £275.

Fraser built a second prototype, the Spider, in 1971, which he described as "a direct development of the theme" of Morgan trikes. It differed only in detail from the AB1 and was offered as a rather more up-market kit by A.T.Fraser Ltd of Sleaford, Lincs, from 1971 onwards at a price of £699.

It's not hard to guess the origins of the ABC Tricar. It was built up on a modified Mini floorpan and provided a very cheap dose of fun for some 25 customers.

Any Mini engine could be used in the 950lb frame of the Spider. Motor tested one example with a tuned 1275S engine, which clocked 96mph and 0-60mph in just 8.7secs. It was certainly great fun to drive, responsive and surprisingly rigid, with a comfortable ride but considerable understeer. A handle was provided on the rump with which the Spider could be swung into tight parking spaces.

Motor said: "It looks like a wooden wardrobe laid on its back. It is supremely responsive and swervable". It won Motor's coveted award as the Most Fun Car of the decade to 1976. Autocar in its test of the Spider said: "The AF Spider is very much better than it at first seems, and the most stable and delightful three-wheeler we have ever driven". Praise indeed.

However, the company was wound up in 1972 with very few cars sold. But from his workshop in Marlborough, Fraser went on to build four examples of a development model called the AF Grand Prix. This was basically of the same style and layout as the Spider but was distinguished by its cycle-type front wings and rounded rear bodywork. The last of the four was built in 1980.

ABC TRICAR

The Auto Body Craft (ABC) Tricar was probably the first-ever road-going Mini-based trike, first seen in 1968. There had been a famous racing trike with Mini power in the early 1960s, but no-one had yet thought of using the set-up with its obvious advantages in stability and handling on a road car. The Kingswinford-based firm was run by Bill Powell and Ken Heather. Powell's 16-year old son Trevor was the intended beneficiary of the car, since three-wheelers could be driven by 16 year-olds. The three men built the prototype using as many Mini parts as possible, and the resulting car was initially referred to as the Trimini.

The whole front end of the Mini was retained, but the rear half was chopped away, except for the floorpan. This was stiffened up and had a special frame welded on to accept half a rear Mini subframe. Then a glassfibre open two-seater body was bonded on top and – viola! – you had an ABC.

ABC would convert your

Above: The very first Mumford, circa 1971. Brian Mumford is in the driving seat. The car's rough-and-ready finish can be gleaned from this picture, while the exhaust looks like it has just come off! Left: A front view of the Mumford Musketeer, featuring its advanced (?) flop-down headlight covers.

Right: A Series 2 Musketeer from the 1980s. The shape was alleged to mimic that of an aircraft's wing for maximum aerodynamic efficiency. Bottom: Holding on... a brave pilot dices with fate at Castle Combe racing circuit.

Mini into a Tricar for £400, with a hood costing extra. As it weighed 4cwt less than a Mini, peformance was extremely good: John Byfield even won his class in one in the 1971 ACU Rally. Later Tricars had all-glassfibre bodywork, and the whole front end would swing forwards for access to the engine. About 25 ABC Tricars were built between 1969 and 1973.

MUMFORD MUSKETEER

One of the strangest of all three-wheelers was the Mumford Musketeer, the brainchild of Brian Mumford

The Musketeer's best angle? Was there such a thing? Below: Bizarre Gilcolt was the only kit car ever to be based on the Reliant Regal chassis.

of Nailsworth, Gloucestershire. Since its first appearance in 1971, it has probably received more bad press than any other three-wheeler.

The Musketeer featured, unusually, a Vauxhall Viva engine, gearbox, front hubs and brakes. Indeed, the Mumford received some publicity from Vauxhall itself, with the Luton-based giant featuring the car in its own journal.

Unlike most three-wheelers of the period, with drive to the wheel or wheels nearest the engine, the Mumford used a Viva propshaft driving the single rear wheel through a specially-made aluminium final drive with no differential and an axle shaft, a unique system which I don't believe worked very well: I remember seeing a Mumford line up at a 1/4 mile drag sprint and dropping the clutch, only to remain stationary while the rear wheel jumped up and down! In construction, the Musketeer was actually quite advanced, with a riveted aluminium monocoque chassis and specially designed and manufactured suspension.

The Musketeer's extraordinary glassfibre body was described as 'Formula Styled Aerodynamic', with an enormously long snout and a correspondingly cut-off tail. Mumford's claim was that the shape was one large aerofoil with a flat undertray to increase downforce. Thereby, remarkable top speed and fuel consumption figures were attainable, said Mumford. The front end was kept low by the expedient of specially-designed suspension turrets.

The headlamps were covered by 'drop-down' GRP panels. You also got a small opening boot, which was neatly divided by the intrusion of the rear wheel. Whatever the charms of the Musketeer were (answers on a postcard, please), it was not very well built with dreadful glassfibre quality and panel fit.

In its brochure, the extraordinary claim made for the Mumford was that "You will be the envy of everybody you pass who will be saying 'There goes a Mumford Musketeer". Fat chance!

The first prototype was running in 1971, but kit production did not start until 1973, when a complete package would cost you £887. This unfortunately co-incided with the three-day week and the introduction of VAT. Only around four cars were sold between 1973 and 1978, after which Mumford concentrated on its sheet metal and trailer business.

The model was revived in 1983 in Series 2 form with some very minor modifications, including a full-width angled boot aperture. But at an all-in kit price of about £1270 plus tax, it was hardly cheap.

Brian Mumford continued to offer the Musketeer (for a while also alongside the Lomax, for which he assumed a manufacturing and marketing role), but takers were few. To date, around six Series 2 Musketeers have been made, and the model remains available today at £740 for a basic kit and about £2300 for a comprehensive package.

GILCOLT

No doubt inspired by the Bond Bug, the Gilcolt was an attempt to create a sporting vehicle on a Reliant Regal chassis. Yes, it's true. It was given birth by the Streatham-based Reliant dealer Ricketts in about 1972.

Its glassfibre bodywork was hardly the prettiest thing you could imagine, with a rather slab-sided appearance. However, potential customers' exotic fantasies were engaged by the curious fitment of gullwing doors. Kits were advertised from £250, or Ricketts would also supply complete cars. It's unlikely that they supplied many in either form.

RANGER CUB

Ranger Automotive was already successfully offering a Moke-style kit based on Austin 1100 parts when it decided to branch out into three-wheelers in July 1974. Operating from a disused cinema in Leigh-on-Sea, Essex, it was one of the few kit car firms which survived the sales crash brought about by the introduction of VAT, and the Ranger Cub trike was the reason, as it was one of the most successful kit-form three-wheelers ever made.

The Cub used the good old Mini front subframe mounted in a 1½ in square-tube space frame chassis. The single rear wheel was suspended by half of the original Mini's suspension.

The body was the Cub's great attraction: designed by Eric Salmons and Alan White, it was definitely unique and even looked quite smart if you squinted at it. It cleverly used a Mini windscreen and headlamps and came in one of six pre-coloured glassfibre finishes. There was a small bonnet providing (not very good) access to the engine, while a boot floor was also available – but only as an option, to keep weight down below the 8cwt limit. A hood was also available.

Introduced at £199 plus VAT, the Cub kit sold reasonably well (at a peak rate of about ten a month). It was even treated to a minor redesign for 1975. Bikers as well as kit car builders were attracted by its charms and about 200 had been built in all by the time Ranger Automotive ceased trading in April 1976. Two prototype models (an electric version and a four-wheeled pick-up) disappeared with it.

Top: Costing less than £200, the Mini based Cub kit was certainly individual and proved popular. Above: Perhaps the Cub should have been a pick-up. As it was, a boot was only available as an extra.

STIMSON SCORCHER

Of all the three-wheelers described in this book, perhaps the one with the most off-the-wall cult following is the Stimson Scorcher. Most trikes are a bit eccentric; the Scorcher is plain insane.

This has a lot to do with its creator, Barrie Stimson, who developed a whole string of bizarre machines during the 1970s, including a Mini-based buggy, a Honda Activan-based leisure car, an amphibious car which looked like a boat on stilts and a 40-foot high plastic pig. His one attempt at a trike was perhaps the most outlandish of all.

Like so many other trikes, the Scorcher used a complete Mini front subframe, but there the similarities ended. On top of the box-shaped tubular chassis sat its unclassifiable, unstressed glassfibre body. It resembled a plastic playground horse, as the

Right: Proving that three could fit on to the Stimson Scorcher, these motorbike racers try the prototype out for size at the Brighton Speed Trials. Below: A bonnet was an optional extra for the seriously insane Scorcher. It hardly made the ugly bugger look any prettier.

Scorcher pilots had to cope with the pedals being split by the centre tunnel and grapple with a gear lever mounted between the legs.

driver and up to two passengers sat astride the central body – the passengers having to hang on to the handles provided, rather like a motorbike. The engine sat exposed above the front air dam, unless you opted for an optional GRP bonnet which covered most of it up. Separate bug-eye headlamps sat atop each swoopy wheel arch.

The driver operated familiar car controls: a gear lever and pedals. However, the clutch was separated from the brake and accelerator by the big central tunnel, so you had to use two Mini pedal assemblies. The handbrake and gear lever were sited on top of the central tunnel, in which was contained a Mini fuel tank. You even got the luxury of a tiny boot at the back.

The whole contraption weighed just 5cwt, so you could truly live up to the name Scorcher when you put your foot down.

Barrie Stimson reckoned you could get 100mph and 60mpg out of his machine with a bog standard 998cc Mini engine fitted. In Autocar's test of the Scorcher in 1976, it was said that top speed was limited by the pressure exerted by the wall of air on your chest, and about 80mph was thought to be comfortable. Autocar expected it to feel like a motorbike, but it didn't – it went round corners with almost no roll, inheriting the Mini's understeer characteristics.

Was it a more a motorbike or a car? No one ever really decided. There was some correspondence with the tax authorities over whether to class it as a motorbike or a car: if it was a car, it had to have seat belts, and there was no possible way the Scorcher could have them. If it was a motorcycle-and-sidecar combination (which the authorities rather unfittingly opted for), then the driver and one passenger had to wear helmets; the other passenger would qualify as the sidecar passenger, and thus need not wear a helmet – but which one should it be? Rather than nark the police, Barrie Stimson always insisted that both passengers wear a helmet.

Offered by Stimson's own Brighton-based company, Noovoh Developments, from 1976, a Scorcher kit could be had for £385 plus VAT for the body, chassis, rear suspension, modified Allegro steering, fascia panel, front seat assembly and four Minilite-style alloy wheels (the spare sat on the rump). Options included a pillion seat, bonnet and a front air dam. Stimson sold about 30 kits before becoming bored with the project, although it remained available up until 1980.

In 1981, the Scorcher looked like it might get a new lease of life after Gerald Pickford of Clanfield, Oxfordshire, bought the project from an emigrating Barrie Stimson, but in the event that was effectively the end of the Scorcher. It is today one of the most avidly sought-after kit cars of any type.

Chapter 6

The Lomax Story

The name Lomax has become synonymous with three-wheelers in the kit car fraternity. It is far and away the most popular kit-form trike made today, or indeed at any time in the past. Cheap, cheery, characterful and unique, it has endeared itself to a generation of enthusiasts.

Nigel Whall has never been a great fan of the Citroen 2CV, but it took an inspired leap of the imagination for him to come up with the idea of creating a kit car using the Deuche floorpan. As it happened, that came about quite by chance.

Whall, who trained as a metallurgist and as a designer for large-area injection mouldings of reinforced plastics, was running a consultancy in glassfibre called Resinject Developments. This specialised in a vacuum-injected system which he had developed and which shared many similarities to the Lotus method which appeared around the same time. One of his triumphs was creating a 32-ton petrol tanker for M&G Tankers which had no steel whatsoever in it.

As he had some spare time, he decided he would

Lomax number one – commonly referred to as 'Genesis' – was a four-wheeler. Here it sits next to a very early three-wheeler.

like to create a lightweight monocoque sports car using his injected moulding process as an advertisement for his company. His intention was to use motorbike parts but it quickly became obvious that substantial modifications to the transmission would be required to make it work in a car. He had neither the time nor the inclination to be bothered with this.

Quite by chance, he went to lunch with a friend who had borrowed his wife's Citroen 2CV for the day. It was misfiring, so the pair had a look under the bonnet. "That was the first time I'd seen under a 2CV bonnet," recalls Whall. "It looked absolutely disgusting. But under all that tin I saw what looked like aluminium cooling fins and I realised this could be the power plant I had been looking for."

The 2CV engine has a common ancestry with BMW motorbike units and looks very much like them, with its air-cooled finned twin pots sticking out proud of the block. Whall realised he could design his car so that the cylinders stuck out at the front, creating a balanced semi-exposed look in the classical Morgan tradition.

He went out and bought a rolled Citroen Ami (mechanically virtually identical to a 2CV) and began to design a car around the mechanical package. At this stage, he was still thinking along the lines of a GRP monocoque. "The first plaster buck looked like a pre-war Morris 8 at the front, so I kicked it in and started again. The problem was the height of the engine, so I had to design the front as close as possible to the engine to get it to look right."

The very first prototype (since dubbed 'Genesis') was a four-wheeler. It used a short

Left: The prototype Lomax 223: this did in fact have four wheels, the rear pair sitting a matter of inches apart. Note the lower front valance panel, a left-over from the days when a monocoque had been planned. Below: Lomax founder Nigel Whall is seen on the right of this picture, leaning against the car used in a 1990 promotion with the Suncharm soft drinks company. This involved some 20 Lomaxes running in convoy from Huddersfield to Paris and back to raise many thousands of pounds for leukemia research.

Above: View from above shows how similar were the front ends of both three-wheeler and four-wheeler. The chassis was shared, too. Below: Privately built Lomaxes were often turned out to extremely high standards. 2CV engines rarely look like this.

wheelbase chassis of Whall's own design, complete with Mini rubber suspension together with the drive train from the Ami. This appeared in 1983, with cyclecar-type styling inspired by the Morgan Super Sports, and in the same year the Lomax Motor Company was formed.

This first Lomax was known as the 224, signifying two cylinders, two seats and four wheels. People were showing a strong interest in buying replicas so he decided to re-engineer the 224 around the Citroen floorpan by lengthening the body by almost a foot.

Again by chance, the organisers of the Lincoln kit car show offered Whall a stand for three cars at a reduced rate. "But I've only got one car," he retorted. Then the cogs began whirring. Why not create a three-wheeler which would attract a lot of attention? It would be easy to effect and

Left: The Lomax cleverly made use of the evocative cooling fins of the Citroen 2CV. Fitting chromed engine parts greatly enhanced the appearance of the car. Below: Another customer built car, this one with full windscreen and doors. Just shows how very differently the cars could turn out.

quick to finish.

With due haste, Whall developed an ingenious inversion of the rear suspension, whereby the trailing arms were removed from the cross-member and replaced the other way round. This meant chopping the ends of the rear chassis rails off, but the result was a car which looked like a trike. In fact, there were four wheels of course, the rear ones with a mere six inch gap between them.

There was a widespread belief that such a system (seen on the Heinkel and Isetta bubble cars) would qualify the car to be classed by the tax authorities as a three-wheeler, but that assumption was wrong. The fallacy seems to have arisen because Isettas were often seen with narrow-gauge twin rear wheels, but three-wheeled versions were developed especially for Britain with its unique licensing quirks.

Following a furore of attention at the Lincoln Showground event, Lomax decided that it, too, would cash in on the tax advantages offered by British laws, and devised a true three-wheeler. The solution was as clever as it was simple: only one of the trailing arms was turned round, but had an extra tubular section welded in to make the wheel sit centrally. The other arm was removed entirely. Because the 2CV family's suspension relies on a single spring for each side coping with both front and rear wheels, the spring on the side without a rear suspension arm had to be 'tied up'.

It followed that this three-wheeled model should be known as the 223. It looked cheeky with its Bugatti-style wheel trims and rounded rump and was the model which most Lomax customers in fact chose (including the author). Building the Lomax was extremely simple as all the mechanicals were left in place and the main body tub bolted directly to the Citroen floorpan. The body was in GRP with a bonded-in plywood floor and a steel frame to carry the steering column and spare wheel mount, plus steel braces for the seat belt mounts. The bonnet and cycle wings were separate GRP items.

The 2CV's 602cc engine developed only 31bhp, but in a car weighing just 8cwt, this was enough to make it an unexpectedly good performer. Few

Opposite: Overhead view shows narrow Morganesque body, which was a simple tub made from glassfibre and wood. The large bonnet lifted off for unrivalled access to the self-contained Citroen power plant. Above: Interiors were left up to individual builders. Citroen GS dials, as fitted here, looked especially smart. MG Midget seats were recommended because of their compact dimensions.

people could believe how well the Lomax handled, either: in this respect, it benefited from the 2CV's limpet-like manners. With only three wheels, body roll could be quite epic, so Lomax advised the fitment of an anti-roll bar, either from the Citroen Ami or using Lomax's own specially-made item.

Before the Lomax 223 was officially launched, Nigel Whall used the services of Peter Bird's Falcon Automotive, who worked on the final production version. This appeared in the autumn of 1983. Peter Bird's input increased cockpit room and made the whole thing look a more professional job. The basic kit price was a remarkably low £495 plus VAT, helped by the fact that no chassis was required in the kit.

By the end of the year, moulding of the GRP bodies was being handled by Falcon Automotive at a new location in Snow Hill, Birmingham, leaving the Lomax Motor Company to handle the sales. Then the moulding work passed to Mumford Engineering, a company that made its own three-wheeler, the Musketeer — see Chapter Five. Indeed, Brian Mumford was the man who contributed a great deal of expertise to the 223's mechanical design. It was he who devised the tubular extension for the rear

Lomax at leisure...

223 ownership meant serious fun and plenty of club social activities. Both factory and owners club organised regular charity runs both at home and abroad.

suspension arm and he who fabricated all of the car's metalwork.

After Mumford had made about 25 Lomaxes during a production cycle which lasted for some $2\frac{1}{2}$ years, most work on the 223 was transferred back to Nigel Whall at his base in Lye, near Birmingham. It was at this point, late in 1986, that a new 50% shareholder joined Lomax Motor Company. David Low had first met Whall when the two men had worked together at M&G Tankers and Low had been fascinated by Whall's plans for the car.

The 223 and its 224 sister now began to motor. Lomax now made most of its own metalwork at its small engineering workshop in Lye, while sales took place from the rented showroom of the nearby Layland Garage. GRP moulding was eventually settled down with Whall's company, Resinject Developments Ltd. in premises at Stourbridge.

After more detail development, the Lomax soon became recognised as a totally viable, cheap and cheerful trike – if not the best quality trike – and it quickly became a best-seller. Three-wheelers were always more popular than four-wheelers (the ratio was in the region of 85/15). The typical customer was a do-it-yourself fanatic who would often make many items himself in the interests of keeping the budget down, with the consequence that few Lomaxes ever looked alike. This was all part of the fun!

Options would eventually include a full windscreen and complete weather protection, fully opening doors and a cut-away in the boat-tailed rear for the fitment of a small rear seat. Soon you could also buy attractive, but expensive, 48-spoke wire wheels designed especially for the three-bolt 2CV hub, plus other goodies like chromed engine items.

There was also the option of basing the Lomax on a Citroen Ami Super chassis, with its 55bhp 1015cc flat four engine and beefed up brakes, in which case a different enclosed front end had to be fitted. Two or three brave customers did build a 423, which corresponds to a three-wheeler with the Ami Super engine – and that was capable of indecent speeds in excess of 100mph!

Eventually Lomax began offering its own ladder frame chassis instead of the 2CV's, which was useful because the Citroen's chassis had a galloping propensity for rusting from the inside out. They even began supplying chassis as replacement items for pukka 2CVs. Lomax also became increasingly involved in the supply of 2CV tuning parts and a front anti-roll bar of Lomax's own manufacture was quickly added to the price lists. The Lye base of the Lomax Motor Company was fast becoming something of a Mecca for Citroen fanatics.

An interesting new direction seemed to present itself when an American serviceman came up to the

Boat tail rear end looked distinctive. There was no opening panel for the (surprisingly large) boot area, which had to be accessed from behind the seats.

Above: The Lomax built by Which Kit? magazine in 1994 and driven with uncharacteristic enthusiasm by its sybaritic editor, Peter Filby, who just happens to be the publisher of this book. The car was the first to be produced by the factory with a two-tone colour finish.

Lomax stand at a show in about 1987. He brought with him a copy of an American magazine called *Super Vee,* detailing vee-twin engines based on American V8s. Two years later, Lomax sent off £2500 to America and received back a fabulous Super Vee engine.

Except it wasn't so fabulous. It was badly made, poorly developed and unreliable, its lubrication system proving especially troublesome. It needed to be stripped three times before its problems were sorted out. When it looked like everything had been fixed, Low and Whall announced their new Lomax

Above: More serious fun. Citroen Specials Club member, David Jupe, corners his 223 at Wiscombe Hillclimb, Devon. Left: Lomax's demonstrator in action at Castle Combe proving its cornering ability. Below: At speed (?) in the Lomax. Despite being phutted along by a mere 30bhp, its light weight meant a top speed of about 90mph was typical. Cornering ability was also something of a revelation.

vee-twin air-cooled engine provided from 90bhp right up to 140bhp, in which case ridiculous performance levels could be expected. The engine could rev happily to 7000rpm, and it drove through a Citroen GS gearbox. Handling was reportedly excellent, as were the torque and performance readily on tap.

However, the Supa Vee was only really developed as a publicity device and has never reached a position where it could be sold to the public. Consequently, only one was ever made, and it looks set for a career in hillclimbing.

Another, more significant, new model was launched at the 1993 London Motor Show: Lomax's latest three-wheeler, the Lambda 3, which was offered alongside all existing models. Although the Lambda could still be built on a 2CV chassis or Lomax's replacement chassis, it was preferable to build it on the purpose-designed frame developed by Lomax for the Lambda. This was a ladder frame unit with much improved rigidity and twin roll-over hoops joined by side intrusion bars – this in turn meant that doors could not be offered if the Lambda chassis was specified.

The most important changes occurred in the

Above: Lomax's own steel tube chassis could be used if your 2CV floorpan was rusty, as it frequently was. This added to the cost but kept weight down. Below: You didn't have to be a total individual to run Lomax, but it helped! This is a suitably attired David Low with a rather basic 224. Note special optional bonnet, which was called the Continental bonnet.

Supa Vee in 1992.

This extraordinary three-wheeler used aluminium and GRP body panels in the same basic style as the 223 but mounted on a lightweight round tube space frame chassis of Lomax's own design. There were coil/spring damper units for the first time on a Lomax, a unique double wishbone system with horizontal coil/spring damper units, designed by trike fanatic and builder Dick Buckland. This anti-dive rising rate system worked extremely well, by all accounts.

But the Supa Vee's most interesting feature was undoubtedly its vee-twin engine: effectively one quarter of an American Chevrolet V8. The 1543cc

Above: Supa Vee! This may look like a fairly normal Lomax, but the Supa Vee was a virtually all-new project with a vee-twin engine, new chassis and suspension, plus aluminium-and-GRP construction. Below: Rear view of Supa Vee shows aluminium lower body and evocative external handbrake.

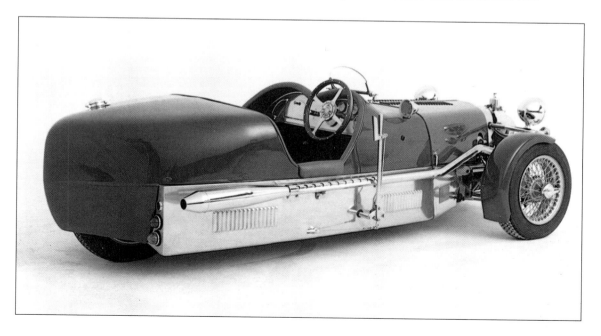

Above: Spaceframe chassis was developed especially for the Supa Vee with input from Dick Buckland. Note horizontal dampers and double wishbones at front and coil/spring damper at the rear. Below: The heart of the Supa Vee: an ingenious vee-twin developed from a Chevrolet V8. Sadly, the unit was to prove hopelessly unreliable and the project was shelved.

suspension department, including ditching the Citroen connected suspension in favour of inboard coil/spring damper units and modified suspension geometry. This cut down considerably on body roll (an unavoidable inheritance of the 2CV suspension system).

The Lambda's body was extensively restyled by freelance designer Jim Dimbleby, notably with flowing front wings which moved with the suspension, rather than with the wheels, plus a new bonnet and a revised interior. There was also, for the first time, carbon fibre strengthening in the body. The whole effect was really very pleasing.

The Lambda was somewhat more costly than the standard-issue 223, lightening customers' wallets by £898 plus tax for the body panel set (as opposed to £698 for the 223). Despite this, about 15% of Lomax sales were Lambdas.

With an excellent model range and a good reputation,

Above: New in 1993: the significantly restyled Lambda 3. Among the many changes were a flowing wing line, new front end and, most importantly, a brand new ladder chassis.

Above: 2CV engine remained at the heart of the Lambda. Note lack of cooling fan, special chromed exhausts, near-flat air filter and phenomenal access to every component. Left: Shape of new wings was penned by Jim Dimbleby. They moved up-and-down with the suspension rather than rotated with the wheels as before.

These three views of the Lambda reflect its up-market image and appearance.

together with new co-director, David Johnson, a trike enthusiast who became involved via his earlier construction of a 223.

Notable Lomax moments in 1994 were the 223's appearance in a TV series called *Frank Stubbs Promotes*, where the car was personal transport of the leading character, a wheeler-dealer played by actor Timothy Spall, and over a series of features in *Which Kit?* magazine, which built one as a workshop project vehicle. Despite one or two problems during construction, the car turned out a great success. As the first factory supplied two-tone example, it looked particularly fine but, predictably enough, its special ability was to create good humour. Referring to both driver and onlookers, *Which Kit?* said: "Making everybody happy is the Lomax's greatest talent."

Clearly, in the ten years or so that Lomaxes have been in production there has been no shortage of enthusiasts wishing to employ that talent. Around 2000 Lomaxes have been sold to date, by far the greater proportion of them being three-wheelers. Many have gone abroad, exports being developed by David Low as soon as he joined the company in 1986. The first two serious agents signed were Automobiltecnik in Germany and Van Den Bergh Imports in Holland. Next came Anton Verhoeve in Belgium, and the 223 now has a thriving market in these three countries, with maybe as much as 25% of production going there.

Spain, America, Denmark and Greece are also taking cars on a regular basis and the annual production rate at the Cradley Heath factory today still runs at a healthy 180-200 units per year. The end of Citroen 2CV production notwithstanding, the future for the Lomax trike looks as safe as it has ever done.

the Lomax Motor Co. was now second only to Reliant as Britain's biggest maker of three-wheelers. In kit car terms, Lomax was far and away the biggest name. Middle 1992 had seen the whole operation at last brought together under one roof – a 20,000 sq.ft. premises at Cradley Heath, near Lye, incorporating full steel and GRP production facilities, stores, showroom, offices and development areas. Sensibly, to ease the financial burden, the place was shared by Resinject Developments.

By now Resinject's production of all sorts of mouldings, including GRP bodies for commercial vehicles, was taking up more and more of Nigel Whall's time and leaving him little opportunity to maintain his involvement with Lomax. The answer was to pass over full control of Lomax to David Low, which took place in June 1994. Today, Low runs the operation very successfully,

Lomax Allsorts...

Such is the individuality enthusiasts put into their 223s, no two cars were ever the same. This page shows in no uncertain terms exactly how varied the cars turned out.

Chapter 7

Triple Explosion

Why did trikes become so popular during the 1980s? It's hard to find an explanation. Perhaps three-wheelers had finally shaken off their dubious reputation as either unstable plastic pigs or bubble cars. Or perhaps people who remembered from their youth the Morgan – in other words, what three-wheelers *should* be like – grew old enough to become nostalgic and want to own a car which looked like a Morgan.

For almost without exception, all three-wheelers offered by a mushrooming clutch of manufacturers were throwbacks to a rose-tinted age of yore when the Morgan Super Sports was what real sports cars were about – an age when three-wheeling was fine and dashing.

The typical trike of the 'boom decade' of the 'eighties came in kit form and more or less copied the Morgan style. There were absolutely no instances of the curiously British layout of a single wheel at the front, as adopted by Reliant and Bond. Kit car manufacturers avoided the layout as if it were leprous, for all the obvious reasons. The pair of wheels was always at the front (where most tricyclists now agreed they should be), with an engine – inevitably exposed – sited between them.

The Triking began the breed in 1978, but by the end of the 1980s, there were half-a-dozen manufacturers offering broadly the same thing and it must be said that they sold far better than the Triking. One of them, Lomax, even claimed to be the largest kit car firm in Britain by the end of the decade.

But there were exceptions: a school which believed that the Morgan's layout was correct, but needed an updated body on top of it: the Hudson Free Spirit and the Triad, for instance. And there were those which aped American approaches like the chopper trike, or the clever mating of a motorcycle rear end with a car-type front to make a mid-engined trike.

At the time of writing, there are around 15 different kit-form trikes to choose from in Britain. Remarkably, if you're looking for a three-wheeler, you probably have more choice now than at any time since the days of the cyclecar in the early part of the century. The big difference is that, today, three-wheelers are bought for enjoyment, not economy.

TRIKING

When the Triking was launched in 1978, it was the only three-wheeler kit car around other than the whacky and very different Stimson Scorcher (see Chapter Five). The Triking launched a whole new generation of trikes which were inspired by the pre-war Morgans.

When draughtsman and Morgan trike fanatic Tony Divey finished his own updated interpretation of the Morgan in autumn 1978, so much interest was shown that early in 1979 he decided to put his vehicle, named the Triking, into limited production at his rural home in Marlingford, Norfolk.

One of the finest three-wheelers ever made: the Triking was as well engineered as it was beautifully detailed.

They're not just a pretty face! Here's the functional side of Trikings with (left) a sticky moment on the Edinburgh Trial in 1994 and (below) action on the Exeter Trial in 1984, with Triking designer Tony Divey behind the wheel and Ian Hyne (who wrote this book's foreword) passengering.

A strong backbone chassis with a steel spaceframe carried stressed alloy body panels with a GRP bonnet, rear section and cycle wings. The whole car measured just 9ft 6in long. The steering was the same rack-and-pinion system as that used on Triumphs, while the wishbone coil spring/damper front suspension used Lotus Esprit uprights. The authentic-looking 18in 40-spoke wire wheels were made by Triking themselves and incorporated light alloy hubs and large 11-inch disc brakes. The drawback was their price – they worked out at over £700 a pair with tyres fitted!

At the back end, the single rear wheel was suspended on a swinging fork and was driven by shaft from an exposed Moto Guzzi Vee-Twin engine. The standard 844cc 68bhp engine endowed the 7cwt car with sizzling performance. But with the 950cc 71bhp Guzzi engine fitted, the figures rose to shattering heights: 121mph and 0-60mph in 7.8 seconds was quoted, although in truth aerodynamics prevented the Triking from reaching a top speed much above 100mph. In its ultimate guise, there was even the option of a tuned 844cc Moto Guzzi Le Mans engine, providing up to 85bhp – and that meant over 240bhp per ton!

Fabulous handling resulted. Gearchanging was delightful thanks to the five-speed Moto Guzzi gearbox with its straight back-and-fore movement. Driving it proved an exciting, if unrefined experience for a tightly squeezed-in pair of passengers, resembling a motorbike in so many ways.

The cost was £4,500 complete, with a supplement of £250 for the 1000cc version. By 1981, Tony Divey had sold 10 cars and customers were given the option to buy the Triking more cheaply in kit form: with an engine, the complete kit-form Triking cost £3780; without it, the price dropped to £2580, both ex tax. The Triking even made an appearance at the 1981 London Motorfair and the name was becoming well-known: cars were sold as far afield as Norway, Australia and the USA. Most Triking production was, in fact, exported.

For 1982, a hood was offered in response to complaints from wives about getting wet. It was a tight-fitting device which clipped on to the slender windscreen rail – indeed, it was so tight that you had to unclip it completely to get in and out! Other options included a walnut dashboard, Connolly leather seats and, later, a tubular steel front subframe (in place of the standard folded steel frame).

The linear motorcycle gearbox was not, of course, fitted with a reverse gear, which provided some problems when manoeuvring. The problem was addressed with the development of an automatic transmission, complete with reverse, offered as an option from 1984, with many of the parts made by Triking themselves. An alternative was to specify a Toyota five-speed 'box, which included reverse. Both options were rather expensive ways of going backwards.

Above: Morgan influence was overwhelming. This rear view of the prototype shows how narrow the car was – ideal for the driver and passenger to get know each other rather better. Below: Constructor Tony Divey at the wheel of Triking number one in 1978. Divey was a Morgan fan keen to bring his passion for trikes to a wider public.

Below: Fabulous looking Moto Guzzi vee-twin engine was completely exposed up front. You could expect over 100mph and 0-60 in 7.8 seconds from the right unit.

Above: Slim, sleek and slippery. Below: That's a squeeze! Optional hood was tiny, if excellently made, and had to be removed to get in and out. Most Triking owners eschewed such fancies as weather protection. Bottom: Another nice engine!

By 1984, the cost of a Triking had risen to £7261. There was clearly a market for something like the Triking, only cheaper, and many competitors arose during the early 1990s. In competition with these cheaper (but perhaps less well-developed) trikes, the Triking looked very expensive for many customers, so in response a basic kit was launched at just £2650 plus VAT.

Without a doubt, the Triking was the best-handling, best-quality and best-designed of the modern Morgan-style trikes, and it commanded universal respect in kit car circles. Its development proceeded through the toughest tests, including unrelenting thrashing by owners and gruelling MCC Classic Trials and track racing. The 100th Triking was built early in 1992, and it remains available at the time of writing, with the most basic kit selling at its lowest level ever – £2160 plus tax.

FALCON

Peter Bird of Falcon Design had already had plenty of involvement with the kit car movement before he launched his own kit cars. He had helped with the

What lay under this strange car which crossed a Lotus Seven with a Morgan? Incredibly, it was a Citroen 2CV floorpan.

construction of Tony Stevens' Reliant-powered Cipher sports car, and helped develop the Lomax for which he actually took on overall responsibility for a time.

In 1984, he launched his own kit car project, the Falcon S. This was a Lotus Seven lookalike, a four-wheeler based, like the Lomax, on a Citroen 2CV floorpan. Eyebrows were raised then, as now, about the logic of having a car which looked like a Lotus but performed like a tin snail...

Two years later, in 1986, there followed a three-wheeled version which retained the Lotus-like front styling but substituted a boat-tail rear end supported by a single rear wheel. The body was of precut plywood panels, bonded together with GRP to form a tub, under which a steel substructure provided strengthening. This tub could be clad in precut aluminium or vinyl, or simply painted. This method of construction obviously took a lot longer than buying a simple GRP tub, but the results were pleasing.

The front wings (either Lotus Seven style or cycle-type), the nose cone, boat-tail and bonnet were all made of GRP and came self-coloured. The Falcon offered rare practicality by incorporating a lockable boot space which could be accessed through an optionally hinging boat-tail. But unlike the four-wheeled Falcon, the trike was a strict two-seater because of the central rear wheel.

In concept, the Falcon trike was very like the

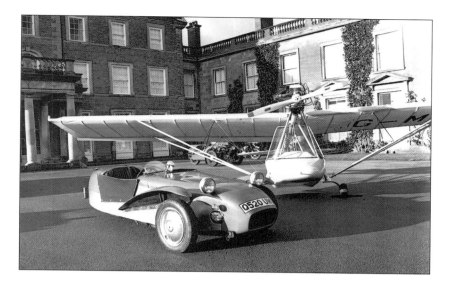

Above: Aluminium, wood and GRP all went to make up the Falcon body. It was consistently one of the cheapest kits available anywhere.

Eventually, Peter Bird passed on the project to a new firm based in Stratford. This continued to offer the Falcon, but the project came up for sale again in late 1993 and was bought by Mike Cooper of the 2CV Centre in Frome, Somerset.

To date, over 200 Falcons have been sold, a good proportion of which are three-wheelers. Kits for the Falcon trike remain available at £2201 for the complete package.

AC DONINGTON

Very little is known about the AC Donington. The author spied it at a kit car show at Santa Pod in 1982, where a notice in its windscreen advised showgoers that if they wanted a replica, it would cost them around £2000.

The Donington was an intriguing Mini-based trike with curvaceous aluminium bodywork which could not have been the result of anything but professional hands. Noteworthy were the very swoopy line of the wings, Mini windscreen, instruments and tail-lights, extremely narrow tail and indented rectangular headlamps.

As nothing more has ever been heard of the Donington, it seems unlikely that any further examples were built.

Lomax, with a basically unmodified Citroen 'A' series chassis providing the basis of a sports cycle-car. Unlike the Lomax, however, the method of obtaining the third rear wheel was more robust: both Citroen arms were removed from the cross-member and replaced by a new structural beam with a suspension arm mounted on to it. Both sides of the unique Citroen linked-spring suspension were then bolted to the beam.

The three-wheeled model was generally known as the Falcon LX-3. The basic kit cost just over £400, and if that was too expensive then Falcon Design would sell you a set of plans for £10 so that you could build your own vehicle from scratch. At the end of 1991, a replacement chassis was made available in much the same style as the Citroen floorpan, but with improved rust-prevention.

The curious aluminium-bodied AC Donington, shot at the Santa Pod kit car show. This was its only known appearance.

BUCKLAND B3

Dick Buckland's B3 was a very strange fish. Despite being widely acknowledged as one of the best three-wheelers ever made, only a handful have ever been sold as the constructor never wished to enter large-scale production with it. That is a great shame, as the B3 has numerous features which confirm it as one of the best.

Dick Buckland was, most predictably, a Morgan trike owner who decided that he could improve on the old Mog. So he took four years creating the Buckland B3, which finally emerged at the Stoneleigh Kit Car Show in 1985.

The B3's chassis was phenomenally strong and painstakingly put together. It consisted of a superbly crafted Zintec steel backbone joined by several cross-members to two side members. At the front end, the

Above: Dick Buckland's B3 trike was widely admired. It used an Escort engine in a brilliantly conceived chassis. Road manners were unimpeachable. Right: Buckland's interior was large by trike standards and featured a removable solid half-tonneau. Below: Ingenious hinging bodywork allowed access to the chassis and major mechanical items. The Buckland was hand-built to exacting standards and remains a very rare sight.

Above: Unmistakeable nose of the Lomax. This example was built as a project vehicle by Peter Filby's Which Kit? magazine. Left: The Lomax 223 was hardly the prettiest three-wheeler ever seen but it struck a chord with a sizeable madcap element in the population.

Right: Triking was the first of many modern interpretations of the Morgan. Below: JZR was also powered by motorbike engines and has proven extremely popular.

Above: Three-wheelers are not often associated with being mean and powerful – but the Grinnall Scorpion was certainly both. Below: Clean, modern profile of the Scorpion made a refreshing change from the league of Morgan lookalikes.

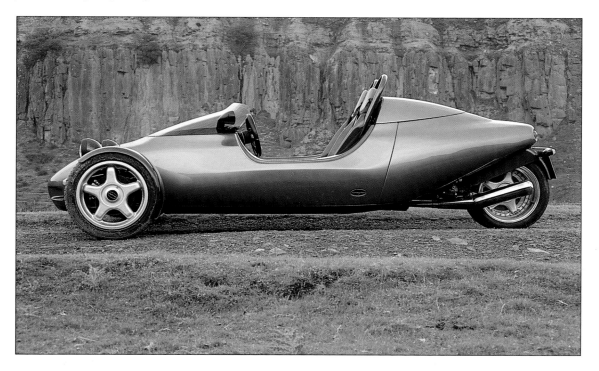

Above: Curious Ghia Cockpit was Ford's idea of a commuter car in 1982. The resemblance to a Messerschmitt was not lost. Right: Dolphin Vortex was one of many innovative American three-wheelers. It was designed for petrol or electric motors.

side members were joined by a folded Zintec frame which housed the front suspension; the engine was designed to stiffen the chassis further.

The B3 was also unusual in its choice of motive power: any Ford Kent could be used, but Dick Buckland used the 1300cc for the sake of lightness. His unit was mildly tuned to provide 95bhp, quite adequate for a very lively turn of speed. Power was transmitted to the single rear wheel, most unusually, through an Escort gearbox via a specially-made propshaft and torque tube to a Reliant crown and pinion and thence to a sprocket and chain.

The original prototype was suspended by front lower wishbones and upper rocking arms connected by Triumph Vitesse uprights, with coil/spring dampers; at the back, there was a swinging arm with coil/spring damping and a tie-rod. In production versions, suspension was by front double wishbones, a set-up which worked admirably well.

Another unique feature was the GRP bodywork. The entire main body tub hinged upwards just aft of the engine to reveal the rear suspension. There was also an attractive one-piece bonnet; this, too, hinged forwards to allow access to the engine and to an aluminium-panelled luggage area (which doubled up as the storage point for the solid GRP half-tonneau).

The total weight of the B3 was kept down to 880lbs, allowing it to fall into the motorcycle tax bracket and to achieve a top speed in the region of 130mph. The Buckland sat very low to the ground and handled with an alacrity which amazed all who drove it.

Only seven chassis were built from Dick Buckland's workshops in Llanwern, Wales, before ill health forced him to put production on pause, but the Buckland B3 eventually returned to production and is available today in body/chassis kit form at £3883.

JZR

A machine tool engineer and car restorer by trade, John Ziemba was also (like so many trike builders) a Morgan owner. He wanted a modern version, so built his own cyclecar based on motorbike parts, and decided to enter production with it from his Darwen, Lancs, works in 1989 under the name JZR (John Ziemba Restoration).

Ziemba's nimble JZR couldn't help but be compared with the Triking: at that time it was the only other Morgan lookalike around. In fact, in sales terms the JZR completely upstaged the Triking, offering its looks, performance and charisma – if not its ultimate

The JZR was a Morgan throwback but on its own terms. Most of all, it brought the opportunity of Morgan-style ownership to a broader market.

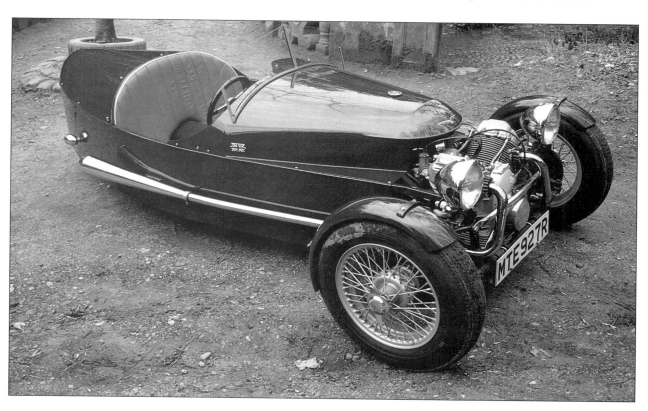

Above: Individual builders added their own interpretations, as this privately built JZR shows. Plain disc wheels, squarish windscreen and individual upholstery prove the point. Above right: A very narrow tail, vintage-style tail lamps and twin exhaust pipes distinguished the pretty JZR.

quality – for a fraction of the price, and it became an instant big seller.

The JZR was based on the Honda CX series motorbike – the first trike to do so – and used the rear section of the Honda frame complete with its rear wheel and swinging arm. This meant that the JZR could usually retain the Honda motorbike registration number and classification. The bike section was mated to a steel square tube chassis with stressed steel side panels and bulkheads. The glassfibre upper rear bodywork and bonnet were then added. You steered through a Ford Escort rack.

The first JZR had a choice of Honda CX500 or CX650 V-twin engines. These water-cooled units offered from 50bhp to 64bhp and drove the single rear wheel via a shaft through a five-speed motorcycle gearbox – therefore no reverse. Performance was still excellent, although the car weighed some 100lbs more than the Triking at 880lbs.

Interior space was limited to say the least and the feeling of the steering wheel so close to the chest was distinctly vintage. Making conditions even more cramped, the drive shaft also dissected the cockpit, being offset towards the driver. However, in 1992 a long cockpit version was launched to alleviate some of the problems of taller drivers. The nimble pedals were machined specially for the JZR.

But it was on price that the JZR really scored. Basic kits sold for well under £1000 and a typical on-the-road price was around £4000, or less if you really tried. That was far below the cost of the Triking and the JZR cleaned up, selling over 160 kits in its first four years.

To bring the JZR even closer to the Triking, a new Moto Guzzi engine option was launched in 1993, in which case the chassis had to be altered to accept the Guzzi rear swinging arm. This option provided more power-hungry owners with the chance to behave like Biggles pilots (up to 95bhp being available to them).

Another option, available from 1992, was a barrel back in place of the rounded rump of the original car. The extended barrel tail permitted the fitment of a spare tyre on the end of it (although you had to choose between a front tyre or rear tyre, as they were

Above: A JZR body under construction clearly shows the square section steel tube frame on to which steel panels were fixed. The centre tunnel covered the shaft drive. Right: Just as cramped in the JZR cockpit as the Triking's, especially for the driver: the offset transmission tunnel is clearly visible.

Some of the engines fitted to JZR's...

Above: Honda CX500 – standard and most common fitment. Below: Honda CX650 with a difference – turbocharging! Top Right: Moto Guzzi Strada 1000cc.

Above: Fearsome 1100cc Honda Pan European V4. Below: Torque your way out of it with a 1340cc Harley!

different sizes).

JZR also built a fearsome machine using an 1100cc Honda V4 Pan European engine. With no less than 105bhp on tap, that gave it a phenomenal power-to-weight ratio of 260bhp per ton. The wheelbase had to be extended by three inches to accommodate the longer swinging arm and bigger rear wheel. The cocktail was explosive: huge power and torque flying through a 160-gauge tyre meant lashings of wheelspin and oversteer in all conditions. Although intended as a one-off, five orders were immediately placed for V4 kits.

The final JZR engine option was no less than a Harley Davidson 1340cc Evolution unit. Despite its massive size and grand parentage, the Harley unit developed a meagre 65bhp. Raw power was not the point of the exercise: more, it was the limitless torque available at most engine speeds and the capability of being tuned to monstrous heights. In this case, a Ford Cortina gearbox was used (at last, a reverse gear!) with a special propshaft and a Honda CX rear fork.

To date, over 250 JZRs have been delivered to customers, putting the marque well and truly in the top flight of current three-wheeler kit cars. Today, the Darwen factory remains extremely busy.

HUDSON

With nearly all trike manufacturers unashamedly aping the 1930s Morgan, the notion of an up-to-date version completely passed everyone by – except, that is, for Roy Webb. He built his Free Spirit in 1989 for his own pleasure but so many people were taken with its unique charms that he was forced to go into production.

The Free Spirit not only looked original, it bucked all convention by offering only one seat, sited centrally: this was a car to get away from everything, and *everyone*. An extremely narrow body was straddled by little rectangular headlamps that looked like spectacles, with cycle winged front wheels sitting some distance from the bonnet. The effect was nothing if not dramatic.

Remove the self-coloured glassfibre body panels and under it all lay Renault 5 parts housed in a straightforward twin rail chassis with a steel panelled floor and bulkhead, plus a square tube frame enclosing

No-one ever said that originality had to be good-looking. The Hudson Free Spirit took that to heart: it was hardly the prettiest trike ever seen, but nothing else approached its barminess.

the driver. Almost all the parts derived from the Renault, including its engine, gearbox, suspension, steering, brakes and so on. Hudson supplied the rear suspension which employed a reversed Renault 5 trailing arm with a coil/spring damper unit.

The cockpit consisted of a single seat with Renault controls in front of the driver, whose only protection from the elements was a meagre Perspex windshield. The gear lever was centrally sited (so you could change with either hand – and suffer lewd comments), while the pedals had to be split either side of the rear housing of the engine. As the car weighed under 400kg, performance was always surprising: with the

Above: The prototype Free Spirit with its designer, Roy Webb. Below: The Hudson's GRP rear section could be removed to reveal the fuel filler and reversed Renault 5 trailing arm and coil/spring damper.

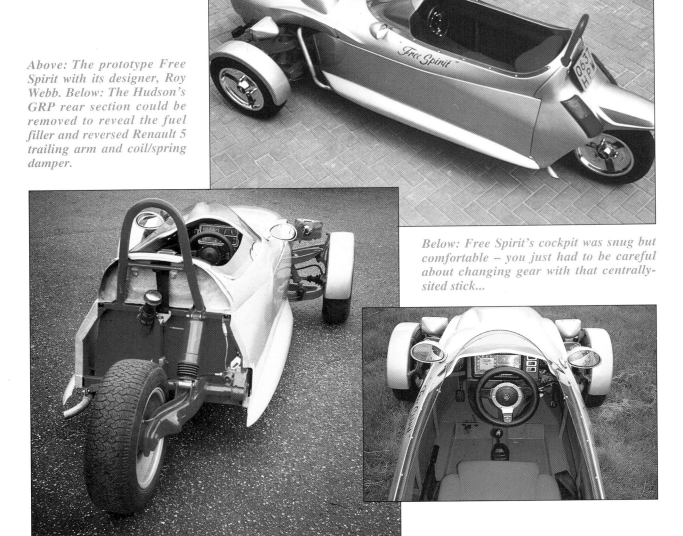

Below: Free Spirit's cockpit was snug but comfortable – you just had to be careful about changing gear with that centrally-sited stick...

top-range Gordini engine fitted, top speeds above 130mph were mentioned...

The prototype was displayed at the Bingley Hall, Stafford, kit car show in spring 1990, where it received a good reception. Within six months, the production line was ready to roll, with a new model also on the price list...

Anyone who condemned the Free Spirit as anti-social got a stiff retort in the form of the new Kindred Spirit. Yes, it was a two-seater version, with the second passenger squeezing behind the driver within the more generous allowances of a wheelbase lengthened by 12 inches. Stubbornly anti-social owners could also liberate the space for luggage – an area completely ignored in the Free Spirit.

In 1993, kits cost £1525 plus tax for the single-seater and £1786 for the two-seater from Hudson Component Cars of Norwich. Bizarrely, when the Hudson passed its German TuV tests, contacts were made with Czech engineers and a large proportion of chassis were henceforth built in the Czech Republic! A further Hudson model was the four-wheeled Mystic, but then that's of little interest to us here.

The Kindred Spirit was by far the most popular, having sold some 140 examples to date compared to around a dozen Free Spirits. A brand new traditional-

style three-wheeler was set to be launched in 1994, to be based on the four-wheeled traditional-style Hudson Rose launched in April 1994. But to date, this potential DRK rival has not materialised because of other commitments. The Spirit continues to be sold today and examples have been exported to America, South Africa, New Zealand and Germany.

Above: Elegantly simple chassis for the Kindred Spirit enclosed the passengers in a cage. Many of the later chassis were built in Czechoslovakia. Below: Far more popular was the tandem two-seater Kindred Spirit, with just enough space to squash in a masochistic passenger.

DRK

DRK was an acronym of this trike's creators, Derek (Callister), Robert (Callister) and Keith (Hamer). Their Renault-based traditional three-wheeler was perhaps not as smooth-looking as many other kit trikes, but it was beautifully built, each kit taking three men a month to finish.

The DRK was unusual in that almost everything was made by the Ellesmere Port based concern, with the exception of the mechanicals. At the time of introduction in 1987, these derived initially from the Renault 4 or 6, but a Renault 5 option was soon introduced, giving a wide span of engine options ranging from a mangy 845cc unit up to the powerful 1300cc Turbo lump.

Each body was painstakingly built up by hand on a hardwood frame using layers of thin plywood clamped into shape, plus a wooden floor. Bonded

Right: DRK's pinched-in tail was made, like the rest of the body, from aluminium-covered wood. Below: If the DRK looked plain, it more than made up for it in the quality of its conception and build. Renault 4/5/6 parts underpinned the trike. These cars were photographed at a kit car show at Capesthorne Hall, Cheshire.

Top: From tiny premises in Ellesmere Port, each DRK was fabricated virtually from the ground up by a three-strong team. The wooden body was painstakingly constructed by hand. Above: Droopy gear lever gives away Renault origins. Interior was more spacious than most motorbike based three-wheelers.

together, this all-wooden body formed a very strong tub which was then encased in thin aluminium, then paint-sprayed.

This fitted on to a metal chassis which accepted all Renault front suspension, plus a Spax coil/over shock for the single rear wheel. The customer's mechanicals tended to be fitted by the factory as part of the 'hand-made' package. A hood was offered by DRK, although it was a very basic transparent affair with roll-up sides.

To drive, the DRK was remarkably civilised compared to most kit trikes. It had a soft Gallic ride, although the power output of a typical Renault 5 engine kept performance well below the range of the average motorbike-powered three-wheeler.

The DRK wasn't cheap, but then it was unique. A typical price was around £2400, which bought you a substantially finished and traditionally built trike. The team which built the DRK kept production levels below the VAT break-off point, so there was commonly a waiting list for them. Even at their leisurely production rate, the DRK team have built close on 50 cars to date.

JBF BOXER

John Fernley's ambition with his JBF Boxer was to create a trike which was cheap and easy to build. It followed the Lomax and Falcon by utilising a 2CV basis, while it used a single rear wheel connected to only one side of the suspension in a layout designed by Fernley himself.

It was a rather larger car than the Lomax, with a long barrel-back tail ending in a mounting for the spare wheel. The materials chosen for the rather inelegant bodywork were plywood and aluminium sheet to enable the DIY builder to minimise his costs. The main tub was formed from sheets of marine ply screwed and glassfibre taped together, then coated in aluminium.

Complete body kits were intended to be offered at around the £2000 mark from 1992 onwards at John Fernley's base in Manchester, but in the event production never began and the one and only car was sold to an enthusiast in Devon.

Below: Rather less pretty than a Lomax (which is saying something), the 2CV-based JBF Boxer had wood-and-aluminium bodywork.

MSR3

Alf Richards was a noted builder of specials, one of which entered production under the name AWR through Classic Images of Purton, near Swindon. This same company also showed an unfinished traditional-style three-wheeler kit at the Stoneleigh Kit Car Show in 1992, which it called the MSR3.

This was a Renault 5 based trike using a very substantial – and heavy – cruciform ladder chassis. Complete Renault front end mechanicals were grafted in, with a modified Renault 5 trailing arm plus coil/over shock at the rear.

The bodywork was classically-styled with a boat-tail rear incorporating a hinged boot lid and was made entirely from GRP, with the exception of the bonnet, a double-hinged aluminium item with an alloy grille surround.

It was planned to sell the MSR3 for around £5000, but nothing more was heard of the company or the project, which may never even have been completed.

Above: When launched, the barrel-tail treatment of the BRA CX3 was unique, although others quickly followed suit. It gave it a distinctive appearance. Below: Offered by well-known kit car manufacturers BRA, the CX3 was very well built, if a little plain. Powered by a Honda 'bike engine, it was comparable with the JZR.

BRA CX3

John Berry and Peter Ibbotson became one of the first AC Cobra replica manufacturers with their BRA 289 as early as 1981. Operating from their Doncaster garage, they developed a successful range of kit cars through the 1980s.

A three-wheeler might seem a radical departure for such a company, but the pair originally met because they both owned Morgan trikes, so it was in fact a quite logical step. Their trike was called the CX3 Super Sports and was launched in 1992. The CX3 was pitched directly into Triking/JZR territory, being based on the Honda CX motorbike, but it cost somewhat more than the JZR at £2200 plus VAT – although the kit was fairly comprehensive. The water-cooled 8-valve CX Vee Twin engine provided very adequate power, delivered at screamingly high revs.

The CX3's distinguishing features were a barrel-tail with a spare wheel attached (although others soon offered the same rear treatment) and a more upright nose with a centre-hinged aluminium bonnet. Only the main body tub came in glassfibre; the rest of the bodywork was in aluminium or sheet steel. Options included wire wheels and hubs, exhausts, seats and aeroscreens.

As 1993 drew to a close, Berry and Ibbotson decided to retire from kit car manufacture and offered all their projects up for sale, including the CX3. By that time, only about four or five cars had been sold. The project remains, at the time of writing, with BRA.

TRIAD

The origins of the Triad go back to the mid-1970s to an obscure kit car called the Mosquito. This completely by-passed the usual channels of kit car marketing (ie. with quarter page adverts in *Hot Car* and *Custom Car*) and was sold by word-of-mouth alone. Hence, very little is known about it.

What we do know is that the Mosquito was a Mini-based open glassfibre-bodied three-wheeler. A strange fish to look at, probably only a half-a-dozen were ever made by a Hereford-based operation between around 1976 and 1977.

Some fifteen years later, the body moulds were rediscovered by Ian Browse and Rick Jones and refurbished and modified so that the moulding came in one piece rather than many separate pieces in the Mosquito. The pair set up in business as Malvern Autocraft, and offered the new three-wheeled car, renamed the Triad, from 1992. Guess what? Jones was a keen Morgan fan and owner – and equally unsurprising was the fact the workshops were based in Malvern, Worcestershire, home of the Morgan.

The Mosquito bodywork was modified somewhat to create the Triad (for instance, changing both front and rear end shapes, swapping the GRP windscreen surround for a flat glass and metal item, and making do without the GRP roll-over bar), but it retained the basic profile and distinctive exterior exhaust pipes of the Mosquito. The front end was all Mini, while the rear consisted of a single Mini trailing arm (with a coil/spring damper) bolted directly to a newly developed steel tube chassis.

For an initial all-in price of £1495, the Triad kit consisted of a jig-built steel space frame chassis and a primered or self-coloured GRP body panel set. There was generous seating for two and a wide variety of options including well-made full weather equipment, a windscreen, lightweight GRP seats, upholstery and so on.

There was also a Warrior version, which was essentially a lightweight Triad designed with competition in mind, particularly hillclimbs. It came with the passenger's side blanked off (though the panel could be removed to accommodate a passenger) and aero screens in place of the windscreen. Although not as popular as the standard Triad, the Warrior did sell a few examples. To date, some 14 kits have been supplied of both types.

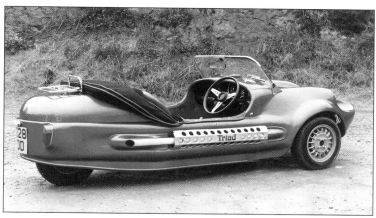

Top: One of the most curious shapes of modern times, the Triad was an old-style fun car reborn for the 1990s. Any Mini engine could be used. Above: Rear view of the Triad was no less weird. Alien-style exhaust was a strong character point. Below: The car on which the Triad was based: the 1977 Mosquito. Differences abound, most notably the weather gear and absence of front spoiler.

Above: Mark Grinnall's amazing Scorpion redefined what three-wheelers were about. Stonking performance, futuristic looks and incredible handling were major features. Right: "Don't bother taking me to your leader. I'm having too much fun". Below: Professional styling from MGA's Steve Harper stood the Scorpion in good stead.

GRINNALL SCORPION

In a world seemingly populated by Morgan lookalikes, the Grinnall Scorpion 3 provided a dramatic tonic. Nothing like it had ever been seen before.

It was the brainchild of Mark Grinnall, who had made a name for himself with his conversions of Triumph TR7s, notably by installing V8 engines. The Scorpion was a radical departure. It followed an American practice of mating a motorcycle rear end with a car-type front end, effectively creating a mid-engined three-wheeler.

The basis of the Scorpion 3 was a BMW K series 'bike (the choice ranged from the K75, through the K100 up to the K1). Grinnall Specialist Cars created its own square section steel tube chassis, to which it mated Ford front suspension (with Cosworth vented disc brakes) and a BMW swinging arm suspended on a coil/spring damper unit. There was full

Above: BMW K series power gave the Scorpion its sting in the tail. With a 120bhp K1 engine fitted (as here), you could beat just about every Ferrari away from the lights. Below: Standard BMW swinging arm and shaft drive fitted into Grinnall's own tubular chassis.

roll-over protection.

The Scorpion stepped into the modern age with its beautifully curved body, the work of Steve Harper of the Midlands-based design house MGA Developments. Made of GRP, it consisted of an inner tub and outer body section, both bonded and rivetted to the chassis.

There was seating for two side-by-side in an exposed cockpit with a small wind deflector. As there was no weather protection, the interior materials were durable, water-proof and without frills. Instruments came from the BMW 'bike. For luggage, you had to stow items in the passenger bay and there was an opening rear lid which gave access to a small removable GRP luggage tray.

With the most basic three-cylinder BMW K75 750cc engine fitted, you had 75bhp on tap. That rose to 90bhp with the K100 four-pot fuel-injected engine and no less than 120bhp with the top-line BMW K1 16V 1100cc fitted. Performance was spectacular in a

Below: Simple interior emphasised the car's down-to-earth performance role. Bottom: Motorbike instrument cluster looked at home at bottom of deep dash. Gear lever appeared conventional but operated on a fore-and-aft gate.

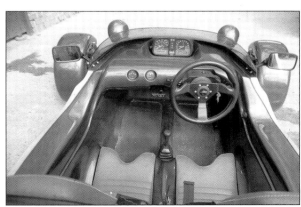

car which weighed a mere 750lbs – Grinnall claimed 0-60mph in 5 seconds for the K100 Scorpion and a top speed of 125mph.

Launched in 1992, the Scorpion 3 received immediate adulation. It handled superbly, with oversteer the predominant characteristic. The BMW motorbike 5-speed gearbox provided all the fun of Formula-1 style gearchanges which were incredibly direct and fast, although the clutch was rather sharp.

Production did not actually begin until the summer of 1993, when you could buy a kit-form Scorpion, minus all BMW components, for £7445. A fully-built car cost from £10,250 – a lot of money for something so impractical, but then motoring journals were happily comparing it with McLaren F1 designer Gordon Murray's £40,000 Rocket sports car. On the options list were a water-proof cockpit cover, electric reverse gear, lightweight chassis (saving some 40kg) and complete weather gear

First lightweight Grinnall Scorpion lost some 40kg in bulk and gained explosive 0-60mph acceleration of 4.5 seconds along with 135mph maximum!

(comprising a taller laminated windscreen, wipers, doors and a hood – still being developed at the time of writing).

The lightweight chassis was standardised in the summer of 1994, leading to even more spectacular performance levels: with the BMW K1 1100cc engine, 0-60mph was down to 4.5 seconds and top speed up to a staggering 135mph. Not only did you have to be fearless to drive such a machine, you also had to be brave enough to fork out around £14,000 +VAT for a CKD (Complete Knock-Down) kit or £8400 +VAT for a full kit less BMW parts. Translate the specification into turn-key form and you were looking at around £17,000 at least.

At the time of writing, Grinnall's 5000sq.ft. of factory space in rural surroundings at Bewdley, Worcestershire, is buzzing with activity. Output of around 30 Scorpions in 1994 created the need for four well-organised, separate manufacturing shops, in which 1995 production is expected to flow smoothly enough to build around 50 cars. Examples are already located in countries all over the world, including Japan and Australia, but Europe (in particular, Germany and Austria) is expected to take the majority of Scorpions in the near future.

HEATHFIELD SLINGSHOT

Peter Heath and Michael Fey's Heathfield Slingshot was another Morganesque 'traditional' three-wheeler along the lines of the JZR. It made its debut at the Bingley Hall, Stafford, Sports & Kit Car Show in March 1993.

A major distinguishing feature was a full 1.5in round-tube space frame chassis, which was extremely robust and featured Cortina front uprights and double wishbone front suspension (using BMW K100 shocks), with a specially-made steel tube hoop-shaped rear arm mated to a Honda rear drum hub. Steering was by Mk2 Escort rack, and the wheels were 15in 60-spoke wires at the front and a specially made 15in steel rear wheel.

Like several other Morgan-style trikes, the Slingshot had a barrel-back body but boasted rather more generous overall dimensions than other similar trikes. In particular, cockpit space was considerably more generous than some other three-wheelers, although there was no provision for luggage (as a safety feature, the fuel tank was placed in the rear). Further strengthening the Slingshot's hand in the comfort stakes was a special adjustable pedal assembly.

The front end incorporated a distinctive hand-formed miniature brass cowl. Construction quality and overall attention to detail were excellent, with such items as a turned and lacquered aluminium dash and leather trim. The standard construction was all-GRP, but there was also an option of all-alloy bodywork.

Like the JZR, the Heathfield used a Honda CX V-twin motorbike engine (500cc or 650cc). Overall weight was 850lbs, well within the 990lbs limits set by the government for trikes, so performance was respectable from the 50bhp to 64bhp units.

Highfield Automotive of Chesterfield offered kits at £2650 plus VAT, somewhat more than the JZR and BRA with which it was bound to compete. But then it always intended to be in a slightly different class.

Top left: An elegantly original interpretation of the Morgan style distinguished the beautifully-constructed Heathfield Slingshot. Below: More substantial than most modern trikes, the Heathfield also offered much more generous accommodation.

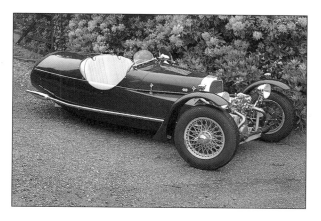

steering column, Morris Ital wheels, Renault 5 radiator and Austin 1100 rear radius arm with a Reliant Robin coil/spring damper unit.

The body was extremely basic and made of wood skinned in aluminium and vinyl. The fold-forward bonnet and front cycle wings were GRP, however, which could be supplied for a very meagre sum. In shape, the body was classical barrel-back, with the spare wheel mounted right on the end.

Despite being intended as a one-off for Ken's use, publicity forced his hand and he began offering sets of plans at £25 from early 1993 – but no kits, since the builder was expected to do just about everything. To date, he has sold 25 such sets, plus a couple of chassis. The expected total build cost was quoted at under £1000.

DRAGONFLY

Built as a one-off and completed in 1994, Bernard Beirne's Dragonfly looked set at the time of writing to become available in kit form. The Dragonfly was unique in recreating almost exactly the form of the F-Type Morgan.

The Z-section steel ladder frame chassis supported sliding pillar front suspension – an exact copy of the original Morgan system – and further enhanced the 1930s feel by borrowing its wheels from the Morris 8. A Hillman Imp steering rack was employed and, at the back end, the rear wheel was suspended on a Honda CX500 swinging arm.

However, there the motorcycle technology stopped. The motive power came from a Reliant Robin 848cc engine and gearbox, connected via the Honda CX shaft drive to power the rear wheel. The very basic bodywork was constructed by skinning a 1/2 inch plywood frame with 22 gauge steel – more Morgan vintage stuff. Completed with details like period bullet sidelights and extremely narrow cycle wings, the Dragonfly was a convincing copy of the early Morgan.

A completed rolling chassis requiring an engine, gearbox and front wheels would cost around £1500, the builder being expected to create the bodywork himself.

Top: Basic nature of the Austin based Trio is evident: this was essentially a plans-built machine with the builder expected to do just about everything. Above: Trio's wooden body was designed to be skinned in aluminium and vinyl.

TRIO

The Trio was the brainchild of Ken Hallett of Wareham, Dorset, but was only ever a part-time project. It used a Mini subframe and A-series engine with a wide cocktail of other parts: Austin 1100 suspension arms (to widen the track by four inches), Metro drive shafts, Austin 1100 disc brakes, Allegro

MORFORD FLYER

The Morford Flyer was first seen at the Stoneleigh kit car show in 1993, where its creators said that replicas could be made for around £2000, if you wanted one.

The bodywork of the prototype was in aluminium glued on to a steel frame. There were no compound curves anywhere on it, so, as you can imagine, it was hardly the most attractive of machines. For a trike, the Morford was unusually large, with a lengthy wheelbase, which at least provided relatively stable road behaviour.

However, retaining the steel tube chassis untouched, the Flyer was being developed into a Mk2 version at the time of writing, featuring much revised bodywork and refined underpinnings.

Mechanical basis was Renault 5, from which almost all the necessary parts were taken. With the Gordini engine fitted, performance was exceptionally good from the lightweight machine. Front suspension was by double wishbones, while the rear end was supported on a Jaguar spring and shock absorber. As for the Mk 2, we shall see...

121

TRISPORT

Totally unique in the history of trikes was the TriSport Scorpion. The project was born in 1990 in the workshops of Bolton based Motorsport Components, manufacturers of components for Formula One and Group C teams. Their idea was to build a modern three-wheeled racer using a Japanese superbike engine.

Taking a Yamaha FZR1000, creators Dennis Aldred and George Holt removed its front forks and simply bolted the unmodified superbike frame to a space frame chassis designed for two front wheels, plus aluminium cladding.

The front suspension was an ingenious pushrod system using a single shock absorber mounted horizontally to rocker arms and interconnected by a Watts linkage. At the rear, ride height was adjusted by special linkages to suit the 14 x 5.5 in single rear wheel.

Above: Formula 3 influences are evident in this shot, but the use of a Yamaha FZR1000 engine was definitely unique. Engineering integrity is readily apparent. Below: The amazing Trisport Scorpion, intended more for racing than road use. Here Formula 3 racer Rob Moore tests the car's brakes in spectacular fashion.

There was space (but only just) for a single passenger sitting virtually on the ground. He faced a Yamaha instrument pod seen through a Midget steering wheel. Pedals were conventional car items, closely spaced, while the gear lever worked on a 'bike-type fore-and-aft movement.

Weighing only 270kg (595lbs) – only 75lbs

heavier than the original 'bike – the Scorpion was a fire-cracker. No figures were ever taken, but Formula Three driver Rob Moore got to within two seconds of the lap record for motorbikes at Snetterton – and that's fast. Top speed was in excess of 145mph.

Traction was excellent and, with virtually no body roll, handling could be fun. At the limit, there were no warning signals and the art of opposite lock had to be finely applied. In the end, it was this characteristic which led its creators to lose interest in the project.

It had been their intention to offer the Scorpion as a low-cost way into racing and to re-open the abandoned single-seater cycle car racing class. With a complete kit set to cost around £4000 and a written-off FZR1000 costing around £2500, the project could have been feasible.

Wahay! The Scorpion proves that all three-wheelers have their limits. Handling problems on a car which was essentially a racing machine eventually sunk the project.

In the event, more interest was shown in having cars for road use. TriSport were quite happy to accommodate them and plans were laid down for offering a road-going kit with cycle wings, indicators and a single headlamp mounted behind a Perspex screen just in front of the cockpit. Donor 'bikes could have included Suzukis and Hondas as well as the Yamaha, but this 120bhp projectile never reached the market. Although it behaved well on road tyres, it did not have the stability to make it a feasible race machine. In the end, the designers simply lost interest in the project – a sad end for one of the most exciting three-wheelers of recent years.

DG PHOENIX

First, there was the 'chopper'. Then there was the chopper trike. This uniquely American phenomenon, a serious cult among its devotees, also made an unlikely appearance in Britain. The idea of long forks and laid-back driving position sounds great for a cruise through the deserts of Utah. Somehow, being stuck in a queue of traffic in the winding streets of Olde Englande with the rain dribbling down your front does not have the same romantic glow.

Nevertheless, the Wellingborough-based firm DG Motors proudly brought the genre to this rain-sweptered isle from around 1983. The layout was classically American: a steel frame, basic glassfibre bodywork, motorbike front forks and a VW Beetle engine out back.

Both two and three-seater versions were on offer. Kits could be tailored to your own particular bent: if you were of the custom brigade, you could opt for a very basic kit and go to town on it. Namby-pambies could buy a complete kit including pedals, seats, wiring, fuel tank and so on for roughly twice the price (£1153 at the time of writing).

Another Beetle-powered chopper trike was also offered by RW Kit Cars during the 1980s, although the company kept so quiet about it that hardly anyone noticed.

Yet another expression of the three-wheeler was the chopper trike, an idea which originated in the USA. A rare British kit was the DG Phoenix, which used a VW rear end mated to a motorbike front.

Bizarre Brooklands Swallow looked almost cute, but was far too heavy to be popular with three-wheeler drivers. Are those really Volvo P1800 rear wings?

BROOKLANDS SWALLOW

This peculiar beast was designed and built by kit car scribe Iain Ayre amid quite a lot of publicity. The idea was to create a 1960s-style trike (and how many of those were there?) based on Mini parts. To this end, the prototype was constructed with cast-offs from other machines: Mini doors and Volvo P1800 rear wings, for instance.

The result was not really how the builder or his intended customers envisaged. For a three-wheeler, the chassis was massively strong, the dimensions grandiloquent (there was space for four passengers) and the use of steel in the construction overly generous. The result was indestructible but far too heavy to reap the rewards of motorbike classification.

Iain Ayre consequently withdrew his Brooklands Swallow into the depths of his garage, awaiting fresh impetus or suggestions as to what to do with it.

SKIP

People build three-wheelers for all number of reasons. J. Jeffrey Calver built his because of his passion for trialling. The car which he created was tailored specifically for this use, although it was equally suited to road use.

The first one popped out of Calver's Durham industrial pneumatics and fabrication works in 1988, christened with the ignominious name Skip. It was based on the Mini, from which it took its floorpan, all its mechanicals and much of its equipment. The space frame chassis was clad in aluminium sheet, topped off with an open GRP body. To get the single rear wheel arrangement, a special rear subframe was built to use a Mini arm with a Spax multi-adjustable gas shock.

Calver immediately scored successes in MCC trials events and sprints. He came first in the Lands End Trial in 1989, the first of a series of wins in various events. Because it was a three-wheeler, it fell into motorcycle classes, allowing it to compete on its own terms.

"My grandfather used to make motorbikes," recalls Calver. "So this is just the next stage on for the family." The Mini engine – it could be any unit from 998cc to 1275cc – sat exposed at the front and the high-level exhaust was a cleverly modified Mini item.

Kits cost £750 to special order only. Included were the chassis, GRP mouldings, rear subframe and fittings. The builder was expected to buy items like the aluminium sheet for the lower body and the Spax shock absorber himself, but completed Skips could still be still built for very little outlay.

At the time of writing, six Skips have been built, most for customers interested in trialling. A new front end is being developed for extra downforce at higher speeds.

Above: Exposed Mini engine gave the unfortunately-named Skip a unique appearance. Body construction was aluminium and GRP. Below: Characterful exhausts on the Skip were actually modified Mini parts. The main intention behind the Skip was use in trials competition.

double-sided swinging arm was suspended by a coil/over shock.

The power source (centrally mounted) could be selected from a number of water-cooled motorbike engines (the radiator being mounted at the front) or diesel or electric units. Drive to the rear wheel could be by shaft, chain or toothed belt.

A curvaceous GRP-and-aluminium body was intended to fit over the chassis, offering tandem seating for two – but this has yet to materialise. At the time of writing, the complete kit was set to cost £2300 plus VAT.

TRIPACER

New in 1994, the Tripacer was, unusually, not sold as a kit. Instead, you were intended to drive to the premises of Classic Car Panels in Frome, Somerset, and have your car converted into a Tripacer.

In this case, as in so many others, the donor vehicle in question was the Citroen 2CV family. On to a modestly modified Citroen floorpan, CCP would construct, over a steel tube frame, a hand-formed aluminium body with an appearance not dissimilar to the Lomax. However, you did get hundreds of genuine louvres and rivets throughout the body. The engine was left almost completely exposed at the front and there were some pleasant touches like shapely front cycle wings and an interesting staggered seating arrangement.

Not only three-wheelers were offered by Classic Car Panels. You could also opt for a four-wheeler or a version with close-set twin rear wheels. The Tripacer is currently available from CCP's small Somerset factory.

Top: Chassis for the DA Mongoose looking promising. It's seen here at the Stoneleigh kit car show in 1994. Above: Projected appearance of DA Mongoose's styling looks pretty exciting too. Below: Tripacer was based on Citroen 2CV floorpan. If you like louvres, you'll love the Tripacer...

DA MONGOOSE

Although still in preparation at the time of writing, the DA Mongoose is scheduled to go into production during 1995. The brainchild of David Arthur, who ran an engineering firm in Warrington, the Mongoose was first shown at the Newark kit car show in June, 1994.

An effective box section space frame chassis incorporated a full roll hoop. Front suspension was by unequal length wishbones with coil/over shocks. There were Cortina hubs and discs and an Escort steering rack. At the rear, a

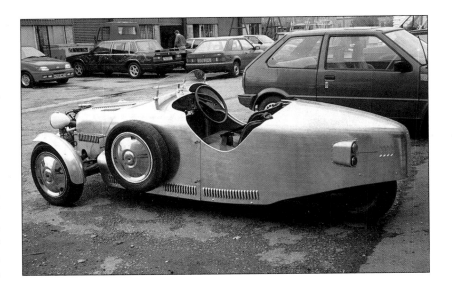

Above: The name Brooke is known for its Rocket-style four-wheelers. But the three-wheeler prototype was, if anything, more attractive to look at. Left: Inside the Brooke: a snug fit, devoid of frills. Note right-hand mounted gear lever.

BROOKE 135

Toby Sutton's dramatic Brooke 245 has become well-known in kit car circles for its Light Car Rocket-style appearance and budget price. Its central driving position and racing-style head fairing gave it an unmistakeable air of a 1950s Formula racing car.

But Sutton's prototype for this car was in fact a three-wheeler. Looking like a bullet on wheels – and indeed being quite the prettiest of all modern three-wheelers – it was a single-seater with a head fairing over the single rear wheel. The 135 tag referred to the number of seats (1), the number of wheels (3) and the fact that the car was based on the mechanical parts of the Renault 5.

The 135 was shown at the 1994 Stoneleigh kit car show but was emphatically not available as a kit. Sutton considered the four-wheeled two-seater version to be far more practical, as indeed it was. The 135 therefore remained a one-off.

Top: Half the total production of Triffids: totally individual Mini-based nutter modules. Above: The Ford Anglia treatment for the rear end actually works well. Cars were built for friends only.

TRIFFID

It's amazing what can be unearthed in the wilds of Great Britain. While on holiday in Norfolk, Citroen Specials Club editor Tom Lucas discovered a hitherto unknown brand of three-wheeler lurking well off the beaten track. Although the Triffid has never been sold as a kit, it warrants inclusion in this chapter because it is too professionally made to be regarded as a special, and because several examples have been built.

The Triffid is the personal brainchild of a self-confessed Mini nutter based in Hopton, near Diss, in Norfolk. He built his Mini-based trike purely as a one-off for his own pleasure but was soon beseiged by requests from friends wanting one too. Rather than cobble them up piecemeal,

he went to all the trouble of having a proper glassfibre mould made up for the main bodyshell by recognised kit car manufacturers Minus Cars, also based in Norfolk.

Since then, a total of four Triffids have been made, including one based on a 1275 GT Mini. They are all highly distinctive with their sharply cut-off bodies, semi-exposed engines and bug-eye headlamps, and are reminiscent of the early days of the kit-built three-wheeler: an absolute basic fun machine. Sadly, the builder had no desire to offer kits or cars to the public.

STINGER

Tony Bradwell's Stinger was a curious mixture of influences, resulting in a car of promising allure. It was based on a BMW 'bike (like the Grinnall), but had a Lotus 7-style front end (which was in fact taken from another kit car called the Sylva Striker).

Built during 1994, the Stinger used a space frame chassis mated to BMW 'bike mechanicals, including the engine, rear wheel, shaft drive and gearbox. At the front end was fitted inboard independent front suspension inspired by the Sylva Striker, while the nose cone was taken from the same source.

The prototype used aluminium side panels, but developments were underway at the time of writing to produce an all-glassfibre bodyshell of a more sculpted appearance. Kit prices were scheduled to start at around £1900 and the first cars were intended to be delivered from Bradwell's Stratford-upon-Avon base during 1995.

BMW-engined Stinger mated performance trike with Lotus 7, and was set to go into production in 1995.

BERKELEY

After the demise late in 1960 of the original Berkeley company, it was left to the Berkeley Enthusiasts Club to keep the marque alive and assist owners in maintaining their cars. This took the form of spares sourcing, social events and helping to develop the various models. Such development particularly concentrated on modifying the T60 models (both three and four-wheeled versions) to accept Mini front subframes and power units.

One Berkeley devotee very much involved with this updating of the T60 was Dave Ratner, who for many years was chairman of the BEC. Running his own small engineering shop, Ratner had a real hands-on approach to the cars and, through obvious contacts, came to acquire the T60 three-wheeler body moulds. Little use was made of the moulds until they were sold in 1991 to another Berkeley enthusiast, Andy Argyle.

Argyle's background involved lots of experience as a professional GRP laminator building powerboats and, in his spare time, as an enthusiastic builder of several kit cars. In 1990 he started his own business making Cosworth-style and M3-style body panels for Ford Sierras and BMWs alongside spare panels for Berkeleys. These were moulded from newly constructed moulds and initially only involved T60 nose and bonnet panels which were supplied to Berkeley Club members.

Once he'd obtained the original T60 moulds, Argyle was able to take the Berkeley side of his business even more seriously, and in 1991 he formed the new generation Berkeley Cars company. Operations took place in 2500sq.ft. workshops in Queniborough, near Leicester, and the business centred initially on sales of replacement body panels and restoration of T60s. Spare parts were soon being shipped to Switzerland and as far afield as the USA, where hungry Berkeley owners were more than grateful for the source of help.

Not surprisingly, Berkeley Cars' business soon progressed, in 1993, to remanufacturing complete body/chassis units for T60 three-wheelers, the chassis for Mini powered examples being made by Dave Ratner's engineering company. This met with unpredictable success. The 1990s Berkeley T60 three-wheeler is built purely to order for either Kawasaki two-stroke 750cc power (with original style front wings) or Mini basis (with flared front wheel arches as per all the modified cars of the 1960s and '70s).

Of approximately 12 new-wave T60 kits turned out so far, some have even been for Citroen 2CV power. A couple of Mini-powered turnkey cars have also been built with the required tubular steel, ladder frame chassis. All motor cycle engined Berkeleys made today follow the original style of construction with folded aluminium inner body panels and floor section, which are bonded into the GRP bodywork to create a very rigid structure.

The current Mini based T60 is called the Bandini after Luigi Bandini, one of Berkeley's works racing drivers in the 1950s. Engine options range from 850cc to 1300cc and the rear end uses a single Mini swinging arm with coil-over shock absorber. Kit prices range from the very basic at £1250 to the comprehensive at £2750, and the range of options includes the original-style hardtop, wire wheels, roll-over bar and D-type style head fairings for the racer image. Your 'modern' T60 can even be supplied with leather upholstery and metallic paint.

No less than fifteen different Berkeleys are in the Queniborough workshop of Berkeley Cars today, either undergoing repair or restoration or as new builds, all of which says much about the new life injected into this famous classic marque.

Below: This is a 1960 Berkeley T60 adapted – like so many Berkeleys – to use Mini power. Owned by Andy Argyle, it uses a Mini Cooper lump. Bottom: New chassis created in 1993 for the Berkeley Bandini, a reborn T60. Engines could come from Mini, Kawasaki or even Citroën 2CV!

'Eighties Escapism...

...took all sorts of forms, illustrated neatly by these machines: weatherproof JZR (above left), daredevil DG Phoenix (above right), sleek Buckland B3 (right) and selection of eight DRKs (below).

Chapter 8

Outer Limits: Extraordinary Production Trikes

Perhaps it is in the nature of three-wheelers that their unusual wheel combination should attract a certain idiosyncratic design element. To rephrase: trikes attract eccentrics. Those whose design genius needs the most outlandish expression possible are drawn to the three-wheeler. Some try to justify their warped logic by pointing to light weight or some such misdirection, but the truth cannot be dodged: these people build three-wheelers because they are weird.

Just how weird is illustrated in this chapter. Most of the extraordinary contraptions you will see here are American. They are strange because most US states do not have a law about what weight three-wheelers have to be to qualify for motorbike status, unlike Britain. So the tendency is towards the truly enormous, with many of these trikes appearing over-engineered by our standards. Some are just plain bizarre, others (like the Sinclair C5) are infamous. None of them is boring.

But weird doesn't have to mean woeful. Many of the odd tripeds in this chapter are some of the most remarkable cars ever made. Judge for yourself.

TEMPO

Surely the vehicle with the longest continuous production record ever, the Tempo has lasted over 60 years to date. This German commercial vehicle is the continental equivalent of the Reliant Ant three-wheeled truck. Tempos can still be seen doing duties on continental roads, despite the fact that German production ceased in the early 1970s.

The first production Tempo was seen as early as 1933 in Hamburg. Despite its considerable size, it was powered by a tiny 198cc single-cylinder engine developing just 7.5bhp, which powered the single front wheel.

All sorts of Tempos were built, from delivery vans to pick-ups, but there were also attempts at passenger versions. The van could be transformed into a sort of 'people carrier' by adding seats in the cargo bay and there was also an abortive two-seater passenger model called the Tempo Troll. A third type was created by converting the rear deck of the pick-up to carry passengers, a variation on the rickshaw theme.

Amazingly, the rights to the Tempo were sold to an Indian firm, Bajaj, which continues to make the Tempo in rickshaw and commercial forms even today.

Three types of Tempo from Germany: pick-up, rickshaw and van. These sizeable machines, in continuous production since 1933, were originally powered by 198cc engines!

Above: Barge-like American Davis was a disaster on the road. Bloated, heavy and massively unstable, it never reached true production. Below right: Fiberfab Scarab was an interesting compact three-wheeler offering the best of car and motorbike worlds. Bottom right: Entire Kawasaki 'bike frame could unbolt from the Scarab's chassis in just over half-an-hour to return to two wheels.

DAVIS

Gary Davis' whale-like three-wheeler was an object lesson in how *not* to design a trike. The fact that it got near to production at all says more for the gullibility of the American public in 1947 than the merits of the Davis: Mr Davis was a publicist, not a car designer. Implausible as it may seem now, the Davis was presented as an advanced, aircraft-inspired, high-technology car. It was frankly a disaster.

The Davis was a massive machine: some 15ft 5ins (4.7m) long and enormously heavy. No-one has ever explained why three wheels were used instead of four, but the net effect of having a single front wheel was to create probably the biggest handling handful since the V12-engined motorbike. Davis claimed that his car would do sharp U-turns at 55mph, but the reality was that the rear driving wheel would lift off the ground and spin freely, indicating a much higher speed on the speedometer!

Far too much of the Davis' weight was positioned over the front wheel and the car was very top-heavy. In subsequent tests, the Davis was found to skitter along its nose on two wheels when the steering was sharply turned at no more than 15mph. Interesting!

The first cars were powered by 2.2-litre 46bhp Hercules four-cylinder engines, but later models came with 2.6-litre 57bhp Continental units. Davis claimed a top speed of 116mph and 30mpg, but again these claims were fanciful – tests indicated 65mph and 28mpg were closer to the mark.

The car was so wide that four people could be seated side-by-side on the single bench seat (again Davis's extravagant claims weighed in at five passengers...). A standard feature was a removable hard top. Some 17 running prototypes were built and the Davis was scheduled to sell at $1400 in 1949 (a rather expensive machine).

But production never did begin despite assurances given to dealers to whom Davis had sold franchises netting around $1 million. This, combined with some financial irregularities, sent Mr Davis to the courts. He got 18 months and was obliged to promise never to re-enter the car business. End of the Davis story.

FIBERFAB SCARAB

Probably America's first kit-form three-wheeler came from the then-leaders in the kit car field, Fiberfab of Bridgeville, Pennsylvania. In the mid-1970s they initiated the idea of the motorbike-based three-wheeler with the Scarab STM (Sports Transport Module).

The concept was ingenious. Everything but the

front forks from a Kawasaki 900 motorbike was used in the Scarab. The entire 'bike frame, complete with the engine and rear wheel, bolted straight into Fiberfab's extremely simple twin-rail chassis. The front end was supported by VW Beetle suspension. The drive train was completely standard motorbike, but a reverse gear was attained by using a starter motor with a friction rubber wheel on the rear wheel.

Over this simple but effective base, customers would fit Fiberfab's three-piece glassfibre body. One of those three pieces was a large flop-forward cab/nose section which provided access for two passengers.

However, the Scarab had one big surprise up its sleeve. In an operation which took just 35 minutes, three wheels could be returned to two. Yes, if you woke up one morning and decided you'd rather travel to work *al fresco,* you could get your spanners out and convert the Scarab back into a Kawasaki motorbike.

This was all a bit too radical for the American public. Despite Fiberfab's offer of kits for $1795, the Scarab was destined never to rival the sales of that other Beetle made by Volkswagen: virtually none were delivered before Fiberfab turned to the lucrative business of making fake MG TDs on VW chassis. Ah well.

TURBO PHANTOM

Perhaps the most dramatic three-wheeler ever made was the Turbo Phantom from California. Being the

Above: Is it a fish, is it a spaceship? No, it's super-trike! Extraordinary Turbo Phantom was powered by a Kawasaki superbike engine and could reach 140mph. Below: Lean, flat profile was almost seven feet wide. Canopy lifted forwards for two passengers to gain entry.

Quincy-Lynn's Trimuter was an unusual little two-seater. It pioneered the art of the plans-built car: indeed, this was the only way to buy one.

brainchild of ex-GM Corvette design studio man, Ronald J Will, it is not altogether surprising that it should come out looking as it did.

The aim was to create an exotic but credible machine for little outlay. Exotic the Turbo Phantom undoubtedly was and, thanks to the sound practice of mating the rear end of a motorbike with a car-type front end, it was also an admirable performer on the road.

Without a doubt, the Phantom's bodywork was its main attraction. Only 44ins high, its dramatic stance was accentuated by a width of nearly 7 feet! Giant aircraft-style air dams, ventilation ducts that looked like gills and a sharply upswept tail made the Phantom look like a cross between a space capsule and a tropical fish. To get into the two-seater cockpit, a huge canopy swung forwards, taking the steering wheel and dash with it. The plastic body was reinforced with rigid urethane foam.

Underneath it all lay a clever combination of car and motorbike technology. The front suspension was based on a widened VW Beetle torsion bar with adjustable air dampers. This was carried by a tubular steel chassis which connected with a single shaft-driven rear wheel.

A choice of Japanese superbike engines was offered, starting with the 999cc 75bhp Honda Goldwing engine, or the same unit fitted with the US-specification Turbo pack producing 110bhp. Thirdly, there was the mighty Kawasaki six-cylinder 1300cc unit complete with turbo which punched out no less than 180bhp! Mated to Honda's five-speed transmission, the Phantom (which weighed under 3/4 ton) was quoted as reaching 109mph, or 131mph under Goldwing power and over 140mph with the Kawasaki

Turbo engine.

From headquarters in Newport Beach, California, Mr Will planned to offer the Phantom fully-built at prices from $16,000. Two prototypes were built in 1978 and the first one was shown at the Los Angeles Auto Expo in April of that year. By the time the Phantom was production-ready, its cost had risen to $19,500.

Maybe it was too expensive; certainly its construction was difficult and costly and it was about as practical as a moon buggy. Disappointing sales persuaded Will to offer the Phantom, from 1981, as a mere set of plans for $20. Only the most adventurous DIY fanatics could possibly have contemplated building up the GRP-and-urethane body from scratch. Sadly, that was the last that was heard of this amazing machine. It is unknown how many were actually built, but it cannot have been more than a tiny handful.

QUINCY-LYNN

Quincy-Lynn Enterprises of Phoenix, Arizona, was one of the great champions of the American eccentric tradition. Founders Robert Quincy Riley and David Lynn were experimenters in the best sense: they created designs and, rather than putting them into production, offered plans so that enthusiasts could recreate them – and that meant creating literally *everything,* including all the bodywork. In its prolific life, the company offered DIY campers, hovercraft, even submarines. But it was also fond of three-wheelers.

The first of these was the Urba Trike of 1978, one of a string of chopper trikes which proliferated in America. Quincy-Lynn's had one big difference: it was powered by electric batteries! Eco-hell's angels are surely a rare breed, but if they existed, the Urba Trike must surely have been the absolute dog's bollocks.

More of a commercial proposition was the Trimuter of 1980, which went on to become the firm's most successful product. Intended as a commuter car, it was a two-seater dart-shaped projectile with a clam-shell canopy for entry, in some ways reminiscent of the Bond Bug. The impression of a space capsule was compounded by the fitment of LED digital instruments instead of dials.

You could opt for either electric power or a 16bhp Briggs & Stratton twin-cylinder engine sited in the tail. Quincy-Lynn claimed a top speed of 60mph and fuel consumption of 60mpg for the Trimuter, which weighed only 900lbs. As there was a stonking 17-gallon fuel tank, sited between the passengers, that gave you enough of a range to get from Land's End to John o' Groats and back to England again without having to stop for fuel – no less than 1020 miles!

Sold as a set of plans for just $15, the Trimuter proved so popular that Quincy-Lynn thought it worthwhile to start a magazine devoted to the car, called *Trimuter News Line*. In less than a year, over 30,000 sets of plans were sold.

The next three-wheeler project was the Tri-Magnum of 1983. Designed by Breck van Kleek, it broke tradition by actually going fast! With a Kawasaki KZ900 rear end bolted to a specially-made chassis, a top speed of 110mph was quoted.

In style, the Tri-Magnum was a sort of teardrop shape with a lift-up canopy for entry to the cockpit. You steered through a tilt-type steering wheel to the twin front wheels, which were suspended on VW parts. A twist-grip allowed you to change through the five-speed 'bike gearbox. As with all Quincy-Lynn products, the Tri-Magnum was sold as a set of plans for $18.25 and a finished machine could be on the road for as little as $2000.

Quincy-Lynn disappeared from the stage in about 1984 but the Tri-Magnum continued to be offered by a firm called, imaginatively, Tri-Magnum of Irvine, California. They said that any motorbike engine from 400cc to 1300cc could be used, but the company folded within a short period.

XK-1

Following in the footsteps of the Quincy-Lynn Trimuter's steps, the XK-1 from Western Front Inc of Texas was developed with help from Quincy-Lynn. It arrived in early 1981.

Above: Sci-fi 'B' movie styling for the California Commuter was claimed to be aerodynamic. 155mpg was a serious claim. Below: XK-1 was a cross between a Bond Bug and a Trimuter. Its engine was rear-mounted.

Its styling was more square, with Bond Bug-type headlamps and a Bond Bug-type canopy for access to two seats. The rear end was described as 'a sloping tail piece with twin bumperettes'. The windscreen came from the Honda Civic, the steering column from the Toyota Celica and the rear suspension from a Datsun. The engine choice ranged from a 16bhp Briggs & Stratton industrial motor up to a VW Beetle unit, mounted in the rear and driving through a Salisbury torque converter.

You could buy a chassis from Western Front or one from Quincy-Lynn, or even build your own to a set of plans. A complete kit, including the glassfibre body, came in at $1695.

CALIFORNIA COMMUTER

Having got bored with projects like setting up Evel Knievel's motorbike stunts and flying an MG from a hot air balloon, partners Doug Malewicki, Richard Long and Gary Cerveny set up a company called Aero Visions Inc in Irvine, California, to develop a single-seater commuting vehicle.

The three-wheeled California Commuter was the result. Based around a Honda 85cc power train, the diminutive Commuter was an exercise in extreme fuel economy. They claimed that the trike could *average* 155mpg, while being capable of reaching 82mph.

The Buck Rogers-style appearance was claimed to be aerodynamically efficient. There was only space for one person, which did limit the vehicle's attractions.

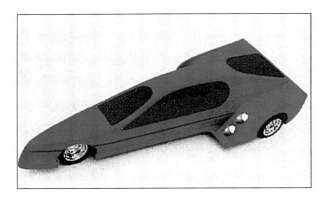

Above: Would you want to do 200mph in this rear-engined three-wheeler? I think not. Opposite page: Indiana Jones meets Millenium Falcon. The Feora would surely have been the perfect machine for Harrison Ford. Designer Chuck Ophorst demonstrates its extraordinary lightness.

It was planned to sell a fully-enclosed version with a flip-up canopy but this never got beyond the planning stage.

VIGILANTE

A most curious car and a most curious story, the Vigilante. It came, most predictably, from California but, despite being in existence for almost 20 years, has not yet made production.

The first prototype was up and running in the late 1970s. It looked something like a slice of cheddar cheese with its razor-sharp nose and wedgey rear. It wasn't very long (two inches shorter than a Mini) and was consequently a lightweight at around 1000lbs.

Construction was a tubular steel space frame chassis with steel side reinforcements, on to which was fitted the double laminated glassfibre body. To get in, you would lift the gullwing door placed on one side; on the other side there was a convertible canopy. Two passengers could squeeze in one behind the other. One strange feature was the positioning of the headlamps and indicators on the rear wings (surely a world first!), because the narrow front end had hardly enough space to fit even the single front wheel.

The mechanical basis was Ford Fiesta, with the rear suspension, engine and gearbox taken from that source and fitted in the tail. The builders stated that you could get 60mpg using the 1.6-litre Fiesta engine and more if you used a smaller transverse power plant from another source.

However, the intended kit never materialised and the project lay dormant until the 1990s, when something remarkable happened. As if it had

previously been a mere wretched grub, the Vigillante was reborn (with an extra 'L' in its name!) as the most spectacular of butterflies. No Fiesta powered economy car now: the new owners of the Vigillante project claimed it to be no less than 'the quickest street legal exotic in the world'.

How about these figures? Top speed *over 200mph*, 0-60mph in *under* 3 seconds, 1g lateral cornering force, under 1500lbs, up to 700bhp and prices starting at $125,000. Ahem. 200mph in a rear-engined trike with the same layout as the Bond 875? Were they insane? Quite possibly because, to date, the claims are pure fantasy. Despite the California-based owners' best intentions, the born-again Vigillante currently exists only as a scale model. Given that the firm is still seeking to find development money, the new Vigillante seems likely never to reach production.

FEORA

Half World War II fighter 'plane, half *Star Wars* out-take, the Feora was one of the most interesting three-wheelers of its time. It was built in about 1982 by a Los Angeles mechanic delightfully called Chuck Ophorst.

Considering this was his first project, the Feora was remarkably advanced. Its drag coefficient was an estimated 0.15, achieved because of its low frontal area, teardrop shape and extreme narrowness. The all-glassfibre bodywork sat atop a complicated space frame chassis and the completed projectile weighed a paltry 505lbs. There was seating for two in tandem, accessed by a folding canopy.

With a 22bhp 175cc Honda twin-cylinder engine installed in the tail, Ophorst claimed a top speed of 92mph and a fuel consumption in excess of 90mpg at a constant 55mph. All three wheels were motorbike items but the steering was rack-and-pinion and brakes were discs all round. It was reportedly a very stable and rapid machine.

A production run of Feoras was considered but rejected because the projected price would have been prohibitive. So sadly the Feora remained a one-off.

TRYLON

It should come as little surprise that the Trylon was the brainchild of a *Star Trek* fanatic. Dale H Fox even called his factory 'Starfleet Headquarters'. He first began his Trylon trike project in 1984. Production of the kit version began in 1989 and in the first five years of production around 250 were sold, including seven in Europe.

Surely the Trylon was the most original and

Above: The Trylon was created by a Star Trek fanatic from a factory called Starfleet Headquarters. Seriously! Right: Clam-shell canopy rose like an inter-galactic star fighter. Could you take the Klingon challenge? Below: You don't expect dials or a steering wheel in a 24th century star-bug do you? Jet boost thruster (aka gear lever) is on the right.

extraordinary three-wheeler of them all. In Fox's own words, it was "designed like a high performance spacecraft, but it drives and handles like an exotic sports car."

Central to the design was the 'clam-shell' canopy which lifted for entry to the tandem two-seater cockpit. The dashboard looked like something from *Battlestar Galactica*, with computer displays and aircraft-style steering controls. The gear lever (or should that be photon phaser control?) sat to the driver's right.

Very narrow at the front and very wide at the rear, the Trylon was based on nothing more galactic than VW Beetle components, including the engine, gearbox, rear suspension and (modified) steering. Its body/chassis construction was very strong: a box section steel cage ready-encased in the GRP bodyshell, with GRP bulkheads, making it very heavy but also very safe. Twin rear hatches allowed access to the engine bay and a useful 8cu ft luggage area. The front suspension was based on motorbike components.

The Trylon was *big* by anyone's standards. It measured 15ft 4ins long although only 43ins high. For a car so long, its weight was kept low, to just 1250lbs, so performance from, for instance, a 1835cc VW engine was claimed to be 120mph, or much more if the optional Mazda RX-7 Turbo engine was fitted.

Two models were offered: the Shuttle and the Viper, the

Above: V8 Motorhead oblivion devil's forks donner und blitzen iron maiden mutha machine. The American Thunder Tryke was for real. Below: That certainly is a Chevrolet small block V8 in there! Don't much fancy the Thunder Tryke's chances on a mini-roundabout in Streatham.

latter including "fender grilles, rear grilles, fin extensions, skirt details and front canard wings" – in other words, a body kit! Kit prices ranged from $6000 to $8000 with fully-built vehicles starting at $16,000, and the Trylon is still available at the time of writing.

AMERICAN THUNDER TRYKE

Hang on to your horned hat! Nothing, not even a date with Ye Byker of Doom, could prepare you for... the American Thunder Tryke. This thunderous Gothic

machine, designed for long, flat and above all *straight* roads. Thanks to the improbably long (4 1/2-foot) chopper front forks, turning tight corners must have been immensely amusing. The attractions of the tandem Tryke (apart from scaring yourself silly) included all the fun of the air, better stability compared with a motorbike and massively robust construction. For safety, the manufacturers added full roll bars, in-board fuel tanks, car disc brakes and four-point harnesses.

A basic chassis kit would cost $4500, with the whole shebang including brakes, suspension and so on retailing at $8495. Complete vehicles were priced from $24,400. Even at those prices, the Thunder Tryke knocked many a biker over the head with its charms and sales were buoyant. It remains available at the time of writing – but only to ye who dare...

DOLPHIN VORTEX

Like the Quincy-Lynn and Turbo Phantom, the Dolphin Vortex was designed to be built from a set of plans. You had to be determined to want one, because that meant fabricating metal subframes, creating a triangulated plywood chassis and covering the lot with a spruce-and-glassfibre body built with your own sweat.

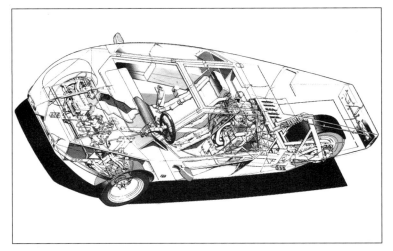

Top: Handsome Dolphin Vortex was designed for electric or internal combustion engines. You had to build everything yourself, though. Above: Sectional view of Vortex shows sound construction, Triumph Spitfire wishbones and four-cylinder Kawasaki 'bike engine.

This daunting task did not deter a band of enthusiasts from leaping in and building their own examples.

Under the front end sat Triumph Spitfire double wishbones with coil/spring dampers, disc brakes and an anti-roll bar. Power could come from any one of a number of motorbikes, the prototype having a four-cylinder Kawasaki 750cc unit. Pumping out 82bhp, this made the 1100lbs car a pretty rapid machine. Drive to the single rear wheel was by Harley-Davidson toothed belt.

Alternatively, you could install an array of eight 12 volt batteries and a 10hp electric motor. In this form, the compact motor drove the rear belt by direct belt drive. A range of 40-80 miles was quoted on a single charge, while a top speed of 60mph could be reached.

Plans sets and a build manual were offered by California-based Dolphin Vehicles for $50 from about 1990. Despite gaining a lot of publicity for the electric-powered version, no more was heard of the Vortex beyond 1993.

chariot had but one purpose: to provide its pilot with a bottomless pit of raw power to sink his throttle hand into.

A bare but massively strong steel frame housed any small block Chevrolet engine (from 4.3 to 6.0 litres!) with a power output of up to 345bhp. Another option on offer was a brand-new 300bhp Corvette LT1 engine. This provided, how shall we say, not inconsiderable performance: one Thunder Tryke was timed from 0-60mph in 3.3 seconds. And even with a mere 175bhp engine fitted, the Tryke could reach the quarter mile in a staggering 12.67 seconds, by which time it was doing 108mph...

The Thunder Tryke was a uniquely American

BADSEY BULLET

Improbable claims are part of the life of small-time manufacturers. Often, it's their only way to get publicity. This certainly worked in the case of Bill Badsey's extraordinary Bullet.

Mr Badsey boldly claimed that his Bullet three-wheeler was capable of reaching 200mph. The obvious riposte is "would *you* do 200mph on three wheels?", but then the world land speed record was held for several years by a three-wheeler, at speeds over 600mph.

The brainchild of Bill Badsey, a South African who had been living in Britain until 1979, the Bullet was constructed in South Africa in 1981. A very sturdy chassis was designed to house much of the rear end of a motorcycle (one of the first trikes to do so), in this case a Suzuki. For motive power, either the GSX1100 or the even more scorching 1300cc six-cylinder were

Above: South African made Badsey Bullet was a three-wheeler devoted to pure performance. Engine came from a Suzuki GSX1100. Below: At speed in the Bullet. Badsey claimed a top speed of 200mph for his trike. Who does he think he's kidding?

quoted. Unusually for this layout, the engine was sited up front, between the passengers' knees, and drove the rear wheel by means of a lengthy chain. Its position helped weight distribution and thereby stability.

You gained entry by flopping forward a canopy on gas struts. The two passengers were separated by a

Above: Badsey's follow-up was the Fun Machine. Yamaha-engined chassis in foreground and, behind it, the completed car/bike cross-over. Below: Designer Carlo Lamattina at the wheel of his BMW K75-powered Modulo trike. Nigel Mansell was apparently a client.

ladder-type chassis with sizeable outriggers, the Fun Machine used a 552cc DOHC Yamaha Vision 'bike engine mounted just behind the front axle line. It powered the single rear wheel via shaft drive.

The driver sat astride the creature and steered via a pair of handlebars to a conventional rack. Front suspension was by lower track control arms, upper rocking arms and coil/spring damper units plus an anti-roll bar, while at the rear a Yamaha Venture swinging arm was used in conjunction with double coil/spring dampers. You even had the luxury of an electric reverse gear.

With its one-piece GRP body in place, the impression was of a three-wheeled motorbike. It weighed just 840lbs (381kg) and was not far off its base motorcycle in terms of performance. Prices started at a much more reasonable $5995. The Fun Machine lived up to its name but it seems unlikely that many were built.

MODULO

In 1988, engineer Carlo Lamattina began work on a high performance three-wheeler from his base near Milan, Italy. Built by his company Italian Car, the Modulo was the result.

A steel tube space frame chassis was clothed with aluminium panels and a carbon fibre-strengthened glassfibre body. Its solidity was proven when it passed

wide central tunnel which contained the drive gear, but made the Bullet rather wide by trike standards.

In 1982, the Bullet was due to be imported to the UK by The Unique Vehicle and Accessory Co of Berkshire, either in kit form (at £4500) or complete (at £6000). But it's believed that no cars ever made it here, and only a tiny handful of examples were ever built in their native South Africa.

From there, it flew to California in 1983, where Bill Badsey Racing USA offered the Bullet from a base in Ventura. Engine choices now encompassed Yamaha Venture, Suzuki GSX 1100cc (105bhp) or even an optional 1.2-litre turbocharged version capable of delivering up to 200bhp. With a price tag of $16,900, it is unlikely that the Americans bit the Bullet any more than the South Africans.

However, Mr Badsey did not give up. He went on to produce the Badsey Fun Machine, another three-wheeler more closely related to a motorbike. Based on a

the German TUV tests. The engine came from the BMW K75 motorbike which produced 75bhp, sufficient to power it to a top speed of 125mph. BMW even agreed to guarantee the power train in the Modulo.

There was a choice of single-seater or tandem two-seater versions and open or enclosed bodywork. In either case, you got pop-up headlamps, a flip-up back end and a flop-forward front end. A major claim to fame was a drive in the Modulo by Nigel Mansell esq, who apparently ordered one as a result. The Modulo was displayed at the 1994 Geneva Salon and remains available at the time of writing.

H-M FREE-WAY

H-M Vehicles of Minnesota created the Free-Way in 1979 as a simple commuter vehicle. In its original guise, it was launched as an electric-only vehicle, but subsequent versions were built with 'gas tanks'.

The Free-Way had a glassfibre hatchback body covering a steel frame and could seat two passengers in tandem. Its unusual shape was claimed to maximise aerodynamic efficiency. Others believed it to be merely the product of warped minds. It was in fact quite long (only five inches shorter than a Mini) and its top speed of 55mph was limited by the car's weight. It was sold for a bargain $2495.

The project was taken on by a bicycle manufacturer called Pedalpower in 1982. It seems to have pedalled into oblivion after this.

WITKAR

Following the Provo group's anti-pollution campaign in the 1960s in Amsterdam, when hundreds of white bicycles were released into the city for people to use freely, there was an attempt to undertake a similar project with electric cars. The so-called Witkars (white cars) were telephone-kiosk shaped, electrically-powered two-seaters. They were run by a central agency and subscribers had access to keys and

Above: This was a brave experiment in Amsterdam to offer cheap, ecological hire transport in the city. The little electric three-wheelers were doomed to a short life. Left: H-M Freeway looked like a sculpted egg on wheels and was intended as an economy commuter vehicle. Below: Quite possibly the simplest car ever made: the French-made Voiture Electronique had just one control for acceleration, braking and steering.

recharging stations. The project worked for a few years, but most people still preferred to use their own smog-inducing cars. Today, a Witkar is a rare and usually neglected-looking sight in Amsterdam.

VOITURE ELECTRONIQUE

La Voiture Electronique is a simple title; but then this French miniature was a simple car, perhaps the simplest ever built. It consisted of little more than a plastic moulded triangle with built-in seats, between which sat a single joystick. This controlled

Above: Infamous Sinclair C5 was a sales disaster. It was hardly the bee's knees for getting about either. Below: Danish-made City-El was a credible and successful attempt at an electric car: it was fairly cheap and reasonably practical.

acceleration, braking and steering, so the car could be driven from either seat – but there was a fool-proof system which stopped the car dead if the driver attempted to do the impossible with his joystick...

Twin Jarrett electric motors drove the rear wheels. The car weighed only 440lbs (200kg), and could reach a top speed of just 15mph (25km/h) over a distance of up to 40 miles (60km).

Built in Moselle, France, from 1968, the simplicity of the concept was diluted as the years elapsed, so that the 1972 'leisure' version, oddly called the Porquerolles, had such luxuries as bumpers, indicators and wing mirrors. The Cab version even had a hard-top! The Jarrett brothers who conceived the car were unable to keep it in production beyond 1976.

SINCLAIR C5

Sir Clive Sinclair should surely have known better. His infamous Sinclair C5, which he financed from his own pocket, was an unmitigated disaster and all but sunk him as an entrepreneur.

The bizarre C5 was a vehicle born of the best intentions but ultimately doomed by the blind optimism of its creators. On paper, the C5 must have seemed like a good idea: it was a truly environment-friendly vehicle, its battery-and-pedal power offered a range of up to 20 miles, it cost only £399 and could be driven legally by 14 year-olds.

The trouble was, it was not exactly driver-friendly. The hapless C5 owner had to sit exposed to the elements, to exhaust fumes and, worst of all, to

advancing juggernauts, with his hands fumbling under his buttocks attempting to steer it. And he had to pedal up hills, as the battery couldn't cope.

Sinclair aimed to produce no less than 100,000 C5s from a Hoover factory within the first year. But things got off to a bad start when it snowed heavily on launch day, in January 1985, and the C5 turned into a toboggan. By February, several local authorities had banned its use amid quite justified fears about driver safety.

In April, production halted "due to a gearbox fault", but it quickly became obvious that disastrously poor sales were the real reason for the stoppage. Sinclair put the project up for sale in June, found no buyer, and so left the receiver to pick up the pieces in October. Only around 8000 had been supplied. Today, the C5 is something of a collector's piece and a little niche in the history of the 20th century is already assured.

CITYCOM CITY-EL

The Danish motor industry is hardly world-famous. The nearest the country has yet come to one of its own comes in a most bizarre form – that of an electric three-wheeler.

The CityCom City-El began its production life in 1987. The basic intention was to provide green transportation at a reasonable cost (most other electric cars were vastly expensive). It didn't matter if it was tiny, basic and uncomfortable – running costs were what mattered.

In appearance, it looked rather like a grown-up Sinclair C5 but in practice it was an awful lot better. Its electric propulsion was superior and its bodywork – available in 'Hatchtop' and 'Cabriolet' versions – was far more substantial, seating one adult and a child in tandem behind. The company quoted a range of about 30 miles.

The firm received a boost when a batch of Mini-Els were ordered for the Barcelona Olympic Games in 1992. Originally it was called the Mini-El, but the name had to be changed to City-El after Rover objected about the use of the name Mini.

The model was even offered in the UK by CCSA Zero Emissions Vehicles, which has to date sold as many as 60 examples. But even as a cheapie, it was still expensive (at around £5500). It also proved that the electric car's day had not yet come – if indeed it ever would.

Above: City-El's canopy hinged forward to allow entry. Below: A pedal-powered tricycle turned car: the Crystal Trice had a tiny 22cc Sachs engine attached to the rear wheel.

CRYSTAL TRICE

Although it does not fit into the three-wheeler categories in this book, the Crystal Trice is worthy of mention. Conceived by the Cornish bicycle manufacturer Crystal Engineering, the Trice was normally a pedal-power only recumbent tricycle.

However, from 1992 the company could fit a tiny Sachs 22cc engine to the rear wheel, principally to help the cyclist to get up steep hills. It was popular on the continent, where laws allowed small engine-powered cycles to be used without a licence. But in Britain, any vehicle with an engine must be taxed, MoT'd and driven with a licence, so there was no market in the UK. A version with ultra-light GRP bodywork was also offered to keep the elements at bay, and this looked somewhat like a miniature Zeppelin. Crystal Engineering continues to offer the Trice at the time of writing.

Chapter 9

Experiments and Design Studies

Three-wheelers may never again be the major force they were in the early part of this century, but that has not prevented many interesting and serious projects by major manufacturers and organisations from coming to fruition. Economy cars, commuter vehicles and electric cars all benefit from having the lightest possible weight, and using only three wheels does save a lot of weight.

With admirable courage, companies like Ford, Volkswagen and BMW have stood up before the inherent prejudice against trikes and built intriguing three-wheeled prototypes. Most were for show, certainly, but they demonstrate that trikes are not beyond the sights of the big boys. Who knows, perhaps one day they may actually productionise a trike.

Alongside the car manufacturers, several design houses have used the novelty of three-wheelers to produce styling exercises. Typically, these come from students looking for an outlandish project to attract the attention of the academic judges, but some major design houses – notably Ghia – have produced their own concepts. Here are a few tasters...

GHIA COCKPIT

A re-invention of the Messerschmitt was what many journalists called the Ghia Cockpit when it was shown at the 1981 Geneva Motor Show. Its narrow body, tandem seating and aircraft-style canopy mimicked the 'Schmitt's layout and even the 12bhp 200cc Piaggio single-cylinder engine sitting in the back was the same size. Only 129in long, the Cockpit was touted as a 'freeway commuter' but no-one seriously thought it had any future. Which of course it didn't.

VOLKSWAGEN SCOOTER

Even Volkswagen dabbled in three-wheelers with the Scooter of 1986. This was really nothing more than a design exercise for VW's junior designers, but the result was credible. Up front sat a VW Polo engine which, in this light frame, enabled a top speed of 125mph. Gullwing doors gave access to a very car-like interior with space for two people sitting side-by-side.

VOLKSWAGEN SM

SM does not stand for sado-masochism, surprisingly enough, but for Sparmobil (which means economy car). And when VW says economy, it means it: this 1983 prototype could travel 1970 miles on a single gallon!

BMW C1

BMW and three-wheelers are not strange bed-partners: first there was the Isetta, then the C1. But they could hardly be more different. The C1, first seen in 1991, used motorcycle technology to create a machine which offered all the advantages of 'biking – compact size, light weight, handling, manoeuvrability – with the convenience and comfort of the car. Although not a runner, the air-cooled flat-twin engine would be 800-1000cc and develop up to 68bhp for a top speed of 125mph. Steering was by handlebars and the body of the machine tilted up to 45 degrees, so bikers should feel at home. But there were also such car-like refinements as a 5-speed gearbox with reverse, a removable hard top and foot-operated brakes.

BOTTGER TRIKE

Unlike the full-size BMW C1, Fritz Bottger's trike remained a 1:3 scale model. Undoubtedly inspired by the BMW, this was a final-term project by an undergraduate at the Art Center in Switzerland. It was designed to tilt into corners and to house a BMW four-cylinder 'bike engine in the tail, although the rear track is much wider than the C1's.

ARZENS EGG *(Right)*

Most people give the credit for being the world's first bubble car to the Iso Isetta of 1953. And indeed it was the first commercially available bubble. But the credit for creating the first bubble shape undoubtedly belongs to a French artist and train designer by the name of Paul Arzens.

Arzens decided to build an electric city car in Paris during the war, in 1942. The car's name, l'Oeuf (which means 'egg'), betrays the very simple design basis of Arzens' car. Its striking body was formed in aluminium and its curved side doors and windscreen were made in Plexiglass – a quite new technique at the time. The result was pure fantasy. Ettore Bugatti was reputed to have seen the Egg in Paris during the war and sought Arzens ought to congratulate him on his 'sculpture'.

Five 250amp batteries powered the Egg via an electric motor sited on the single-wheel trailing arm. This gave it a range of 60 miles at 45mph. The Egg

never went into production but it still exists today, now fitted with a 125cc petrol engine, and was until recently in the hands of its inventor. He died in 1990, aged 87.

CHEVROLET ASTRO III

More fanciful was Chevrolet's Astro III of 1969. This, too, had a lift-up canopy, single front wheel and seating for two, but it was no more than a non-running interstellar pod for display at shows. The intended powerplant was no less than a jet turbine.

DAIHATSU BC-7 *(Right)*

Short and green – that was the message behind the BC-7, Daihatsu's 1989 moped-turned-electric-bubble. There was only one seat and the driver steered using handlebars.

GM 511

This sporty-looking trike was an anomaly built by General Motors in the late 1960s. It featured a large forward-opening canopy, seating for two and an overall height of just 40 inches, which reportedly helped its stability. Fitted with an 1100cc engine and 3-speed gearbox, it was claimed to reach 80mph.

BSA LADYBIRD

Apart from its motorbikes, BSA is most famous for the three-wheelers it made before the war. They rivalled Morgan's trikes and featured front-wheel drive. BSA might have returned as a car manufacturer if the Ladybird prototype had been given the go-ahead. It was built in 1960 with a Triumph Tigress 250cc vertical twin engine. The extremely compact open two-seater body was hand-made from a single sheet of steel. However, it was not approved for production and the Ladybird was the last car BSA ever built. It is now in the hands of a microcar collector.

LEPOIX DING

Louis Lepoix's electrically-propelled Ding was a debutant at the 1975 Frankfurt Motor Show (Lepoix was based in Baden Baden, Germany). This was one of the most lunatic creations ever to grace the road. Its most striking feature was an extraordinary external chassis which looped up and around the glassfibre body which sat suspended in the middle of it. Together with the three bubble-form wheels, the impression given was of a refugee from a science-fiction film set.

The rear wheels were powered by a 1.5kW 24-volt motor and the batteries sat under the two seats. Hardly intended as a barn-storming thunder-wagon, its top speed was a mere 16mph.

Alas, the Ding was never to reach intended production in 1977. The author can only express his regret that the public was not ready for such a prodigy.

TRIPOD

The Tripod might have joined the Bamby and Cursor as one of Britain's rare modern production microcars, but sadly it never even got the chance to try. It was the brainchild of Dennis Rowans, managing director of the UK's Suzuki importers, Heron.

Work began in 1985 to create a weatherproof alternative to a moped. The intention was to create a viable means of transport to cost under £1200, using Suzuki moped parts so that Type Approval would not be required.

John Mockett designed the Tripod with two wheels at the front and a single wheel to the rear. It used an advanced aluminium honeycomb chassis (as used on Grand Prix motorbikes) – strong, light, yet easy to make. The two-seater bodywork was in GRP.

Some five or six working prototypes were built between 1986 and 1987 and fully tested at MIRA with the support of the Department of Transport. The Tripod was pronounced roadworthy and very safe.

The Tripod was to be made at a new factory by Heron, but the costings of the project killed it. The projected price spiralled to the extent where it would have cost upwards of £2000, and there was little leeway to cut costs. Heron conducted test marketing and found that customers believed the Tripod did not have that perceived value. So despite appearances on *Top Gear* and in the *Daily Mail,* the Tripod trod no more. In fact, it was trodden on, as all the prototypes were, sadly, subsequently crushed.

JEPHCOTT MICRO

Engineer Dr. Jephcott obviously had a Mr Hyde as well. His 1984 leaning car pioneered the use of technology which made it behave like a motorcycle around bends. With a smart body designed by Richard Oakes, there were noises about taking the project further. As it was, it simply faded away, although it was displayed for nine weeks at the London Design Centre.

GM LEAN MACHINE *(Right)*

In an almost spooky co-incidence, GM produced at around the same time as Jephcott's a car called the Lean Machine. Guess what? It leaned into corners. It was powered by a 30bhp Honda 'bike engine. Fittingly, it made its debut at Disneyland – and promptly returned to Never-Never-Land.

FASCINATION *(Left)*

Possibly the largest three-wheeler ever made was the 1971 American Fascination, designed by Paul Lewis who had previously built the Lewis Airmobile three-wheeler in 1937. It was an incredible 5.2m (over 17ft) long – that's bigger than a Rolls-Royce but was claimed to weigh only 815kg (1796lb). Its teardrop glassfibre body could seat five and had all-enveloping bumpers. None of the windows opened, so air conditioning was standard. A 70bhp Renault 16 engine powered this amazing beast, which was set to be made by the Highway Aircraft Corp. Alas and inevitably, it never was.

PPV

The precursor to those Mediterranean pedalos, the 1973 Californian PPV (People Powered Vehicle) had this additional benefit: parking on end! A version was offered in France with a small petrol engine under the name Petit Puce (Little Flea).

MINK *(Below)*

This little UFO saucer is called the Mink and could have become the only car ever made in Bermuda. The prototype was built in Britain in 1968 with a 200cc Lambretta engine. Its preposterous front overhang gave it spectacularly unbalanced road behaviour and the prototype remained unique.

FORD VOLANTE *(Below)*

A three-wheeler that can fly? No lesser an organisation than Ford claimed as much with their Volante of 1961. Of this non-functioning scale model Ford bafflingly stated: "The tri-athodyne concept calls for ultra-sophisticated use of the ducted fan principle, employed in a unique manner". Can anyone smell cowpats?

Chapter 10

Out-Takes & One-Offs

If you thought that was the end of it, well so did the author and the publisher. But during the preparation of this book, the sheer and astonishing volume and variety of three-wheelers led them to create this little dustbin of out-takes.

There is no logic to this chapter. Just about anything is valid for inclusion – if we liked the look of it or if it made us laugh, we put it in.

If nothing else, this chapter gives some clue as to just how vast is the world of machines with one wheel missing. Unhinged, implausible, unstable, inconceivable – they are all here. We hope you will enjoy them as much we have.

Above: This cute Puch moped-powered projectile is the Meister G5N, made in Austria in 1969. Although dismally slow, it provided a smidgen of weather protection, seating for two and a sort of giant handkerchief as a hatchback.

Above: Is that a Bugatti grille I see before me? Well actually, yes. This 125cc microcar, called the OTI, had a strong right to wear the Bugatti horseshoe since it was built at the old Bugatti works in Molsheim in 1959. How the mighty are fallen... Right: A very rare Felber Autoroller, made by one of a tiny handful of Austrian manufacturers. Its 398cc engine was rear-mounted and developed 15bhp. Probably around 400 Felbers were made between 1952 and 1954 and this is one of only two known survivors.

Above: The brilliantly-named Sulky was made by the Italian firm Casalini. It had a moped engine, steel bodywork and seating for two. First seen in 1975, it has remained a consistent part of the Italian motoring scene right up to today. Below: Land ahoy! The amazing Inter was a French equivalent of the Messerschmitt. It too was made by an aeroplane manufacturer from 1953 and had a small (175cc) engine. The front wheels folded up under the car to make it even narrower!

Top: A rare picture of the Hungarian Meray, made by a firm better known for its motorbikes. Built between 1928 and 1932, the Meray had a rear-mounted 500cc JAP engine. Here co-founder Endre Meray-Horvath is seen standing by his creation. Above: The German-made Fuldamobil was known in its native land as the Silver Flea. The engine was a 191cc single-cylinder unit and the bodywork was first in aluminium, later in glassfibre. Production lasted from 1951 to 1969. Below: This monstrosity was spied 'for sale' at the 1993 Stoneleigh kit car show. Identity is unknown, although it looks like it is based on a Morris 1100.

Left: New York, New York! Particularly brave travellers in 1979 could opt to dodge the Dodges and check out the Checkers in The Big Apple in this curious moped-engined trike called the Tri-Ped Microcar.

Below: Britain's Finest Three-Wheeler was a steep claim for the Gordon, one of the crudest of the economy tricycles in the 1950s. Note the eccentrically-positioned 197cc engine covered by a blister in the bodywork.

DHE 5402

Above: Under this disastrously ugly and appallingly-made glassfibre body is an Indian-built chassis and 198cc single-cylinder engine. The car is called the Sunrise Badal and was made in Bangalore 1978-82. The same manufacturer is now building Austin Montegos in India! Below: Peter Hill's special (nicknamed the Yellow Peril) is based on a Citroen Dyane chassis with a rear wheel conversion done by a local welder, which retains both sides of the suspension. The bodywork is sheet aluminium on a steel frame, except for the front cowl which is a hot water cylinder! The car took part in the 1993 Stella Alpine Rally in Italy – not bad for a car which cost only £450 to build.

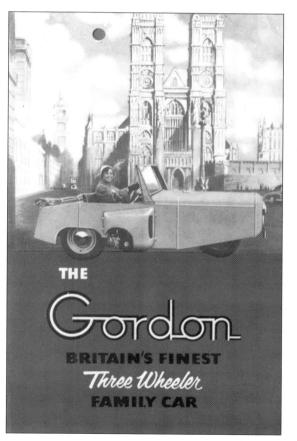

THE

Gordon

BRITAIN'S FINEST
Three Wheeler
FAMILY CAR

ELX 655T

Left: Wasp-like Suntera SunRay is made in Hawaii and is apparently used by Hawaiian police – book him Danno. This solar-electric two-seater's rotating doors double up as bullet-proof riot shields – no kidding! Below: This is a Tourette made by the British firm Progress Supreme in 1957. Powered by a tiny 197cc engine, it was capable of reaching no less than 55mph. Note the flop-forward hard top. Only 26 Tourettes were made.

Below: The Swiss-made Twike is designed as a weatherproof tricycle. As well as an electric motor, both passengers are supplied with pedals for the ultimate in ecological transportation.

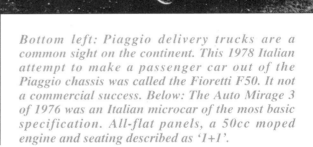

Bottom left: Piaggio delivery trucks are a common sight on the continent. This 1978 Italian attempt to make a passenger car out of the Piaggio chassis was called the Fioretti F50. It not a commercial success. Below: The Auto Mirage 3 of 1976 was an Italian microcar of the most basic specification. All-flat panels, a 50cc moped engine and seating described as '1+1'.

Right: This weird one-off owes more than a little of its inspiration to the Stimson Scorcher (see Chapter Five). Something Special uses Mini mechanicals in a home-built frame clothed with sheet metal. The bizarre wind deflector is in fact a Perspex telephone booth cover.

Left: Prototype of unknown origin which appears to be sponsored by BaByliss and powered by a Lombardini engine. Possibly an economy special, almost certainly designed by an amateur. Below: Presented as 'the automobile in touch with tomorrow', the Ceres was claimed to have a Cd figure of just 0.18. Powered by a rear-mounted Daihatsu Charade engine, the American-built Ceres cost $14,000 in 1983.

Left: This creation was called 'Moonshine Madness' and was built in 1972 by leading hot rodder, Ray Christopher, as a publicity wagon for a whisky company. Yes, that's a sofa tucked into the bodywork and yes, that's a beer barrel above the Hillman Imp engine. Juding by those castors on the tail, the driver expected to do wheelies!

Right: This metal-bodied home-made trike appears to hark back to the days of the dual-cowl landaulette. The rear passengers get a windscreen and a hood! Below: Curious trike seen at the 1993 National Microcar Rally. Moped parts have been bolted into a basic chassis with a minimum of bodywork attached. Note the exposed fuel tank in front of the passenger's knees.

Below: Richard Martin built his Martini in six months on a budget of £370 so that he could enter the National Motor Cycle Rally. Everything was scratch built on a Citroen Dyane chassis, with a single rear suspension arm. It has such luxuries as doors, a roll-over bar and full windscreen at the insistence of the 'navigator', Mrs Martin.

Above: Styling exercise of unknown origin. Lettering says 'PSA', suggesting perhaps a Peugeot sponsorship. Engine is front-mounted and drive is to the front wheels. Below: This 2CV based trike has only one seat. To move the steering wheel six inches towards the centre of the car, builder Philip Barlow had to use two universal joints. The narrow (32.5in) body is made from aluminium over a steel frame, bolted through a plywood floor to the Citroen floorpan. The bulge in the bonnet has nothing to do with power – the spare wheel is mounted beside the driver's feet!

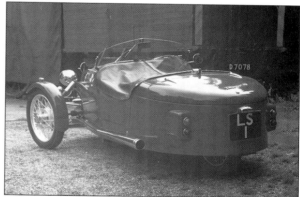

Above: One of the most professional one-off trikes ever built, the Trilux cleverly used Citroen Ami bits in a home-made chassis. Parts included Morris Marina steering rack and torque bars, Renault 12 swivel joints fitted to Citroen drive shafts, Austin Seven 19in wheels, Mazda RX7-derived front wishbones and Ami-based rear suspension. A remote gearchange was made to mate with the Ami 'box. The very handsome bodywork is in aluminium sheet over a steel tube frame, with GRP bonnet, hinging boot lid, rear light mountings and alternator belt cover. The constructor, who completed the Trilux in 1986, entertained the possibility of kit production, but the projected price would have been too high.

Right: Wonderful Fuji Cabin was a 1957 vintage city car from Tokyo. Its plastic body looked like a boiled egg and it could transport two people at speeds up to 37mph. Some 85 examples were made. Below: The empire which is Daihatsu was founded on three-wheelers like this Midget from the 1950s. Obviously inspired by the Piaggio, it was sold in a variety of body styles including rickshaws, vans and station wagons.

WAGON TYPE

Above: Monumentally ugly Meyra 200 was pretty big for a 198cc trike: some 136in (345cm) long. You got in through a single door which opened at the front of the car. Mystifyingly, almost 500 of these monstrosities were built in Germany between 1955 and 1956. Left: Citroën '2CV3' was created by the author as a bit of a joke, but it did actually run – in a spectacularly wayward fashion. Perhaps fortunately, it has now been scrapped.

This and following page: A panorama of Citroën 2CV based specials. The ease of building a unique home-made body on a 2CV chassis has attracted dozens of amateurs to create their own individual machines. The Citroën chassis lends itself particularly well to having one rear wheel removed. A special club, the Citroën Specials Club, has been formed to cater for the ever-widening variety of these madcap machines. ▶

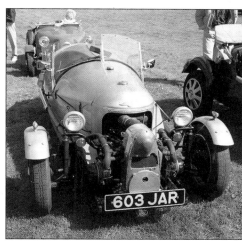

An A-Z of Three-Wheelers

Not every three-wheeler made it into the main part of this book. There have been literally hundreds of minor marques producing a broad variety of designs from 1885 to the present day. For reference purposes and the sake of completeness, the following A to Z attempts to list all known three-wheelers. Included is every three-wheeler which was actually produced or intended for production. In general, certain categories such as commercial vehicles, two-wheeled vehicles, powered 'wheels', invalid carriages and one-off specials are excluded.

Key to Countries

A	= Austria	GB	= Great Britain	RC	= Taiwan
AUS	= Australia	GBM	= Isle of Man	RCH	= Chile
B	= Belgium	GR	= Greece	RI	= Indonesia
CDN	= Canada	H	= Hungary	RSM	= San Marino
CH	= Switzerland	I	= Italy	S	= Sweden
CS	= Czechoslovakia	IND	= India	SU	= Russia
D	= Germany	IRL	= Ireland	USA	= United States
DK	= Denmark	J	= Japan		of America
E	= Spain	MA	= Morocco	VN	= Vietnam
F	= France	NL	= Netherlands	ZA	= South Africa

	Dates of Manufacture	Country of Origin
AB1	1971	GB
ABC	1971	GB
AC Donington	1982	GB
AC Sociable	1908-14	GB
AC Petite	1953-58	GB
ACAM Nica	1984-87	I
Acoma Mini-Comtesse	1976-80	F
ADI	1950	D
Aerocarene	1947	F
AF Spider	1971-72	GB
AF Grand Prix	1972-80	GB
Albrecht	1950-51	D
Aleu	1954	E
Allard Clipper	1953-c55	GB
All Cars Charly	1974-85	I
Alta	1968-77	GR
American Thunder Tryke	1993-date	USA
American Tri-Car	1912	USA
Andre Py	1899	F
API Rickshaw	1955-date	IND
Argeo	1925	D
Armadale	1906-07	GB
Arola	1976-83	F
Arzens l'Oeuf	1942	F
Atomette	1922	GB
Attica	1964-68	GR
Autocar	1897	USA
Autogear	1922-23	GB
Automirage Mirage 3	1976-85	I
Automotette	1898-99	F
Auto Riksha	1980s	IND
Auto Tri-Car	1914	USA
Autotrix	1913	GB
Avolette	1955-58	F
Avon Trimobile	1903-10	GB
Badsey Bullet	c1979-83	ZA/USA
Fun Machine	1980s	USA
Bajaj	1960s-date	IND
Baldet Bluebird	1950s	GB
Bambi	1960s	RCH
Bamby	1983-84	GB
Barnes	1904-06	GB
Barrows	1897-88	USA
Basson's Star	1956	USA
Bat	1904-09	GB
Beeston	1898-99	GB
BEF	1907-13	D
Belcar	1955-c56	CH
Bell	1920	GB
Bel-Motors Veloto	1976-81	F
Benz	1885-95	D
Bergemann	1953	D
Berkeley T60	1959-60	GB
Berkeley Bandini	1991-date	GB
Bernardi	1899-1901	I
Blohm & Voss	1945-46	D
BMA Amica	1971-80	I
BMA Brio	1978-86	I
BMA Nuova Amica	1980-date	I
BMW Isetta	1955-62	D
Bond Minicar	1949-66	GB
Bond 875	1965-70	GB
Bond Bug	1970-74	GB
Boselli	1952	I
Bouffort	1951-60	F
BRA CX3	1992-date	GB
Bramham	1922-24	GB
Bramwell-Robinson	1899-1901	USA
Brissonet Roulante	1953	F
Brogan	1946-48	USA
Brooke	1993	GB
Brooklands Swallow	1993	GB
Brutsch 200 Spatz	1954	D
Brutsch Zwerg	1955-57	D
Brutsch Mopetta	1956-58	D
Brutsch Rollera	1956-58	D
Brutsch Bussard	1956-58	D
BSA	1929-36	GB
BSA Ladybird	1960	GB
Bubu Cabinscooter	1982	J
Buckland B3	1985-date	GB
Bully	1933	D
Bunger	1947-49	DK
Butler	1887	GB
Californian Commuter	1985	USA
Cambro	1920	GB
Canadian Motor Synd	1895-89	CDN
Carpeviam	1903-05	GB
Casalini Sulky	1975-date	I
Castle Three	1919-22	GB
CEDRE	1974-87	F
Century	1899-1901	GB
Ceres	1983	USA
Cheetah	1992-date	CH
CIMEM Girino	1951	I
Cingolani	1952	I
CityCom City-El	1987-date	DK
Classic Images MSR3	1992	GB
Cloumobil	1906-08	D
Colliday	1960s	GB
Colombo	1922-24	I
Comet	1946-48	USA
Comet	1950-51	USA
Condor	1913	GB
Convenient Machines Cub	1982-83	USA
Corat Lupetta	1946	I
Coronet	1957-60	GB
Coventry-Victor	1926-38	GB
Crouch	1912-13	GB
Crown	1903	GB
Crystal Sachs Trice	1992-date	GB
Csonka	1906	H
Cursor	1985-87	GB
Cushman	1982	USA
Custer Electric Chair	1930s	USA
Cyclauto	1919-23	F
Cyklon	1902-29	D
DA Mongoose	1994-date	GB
Daihatsu Bee	1950s	J
Midget/Tri-Mobile	1950s	J
Dallison	1913	GB
Dandey	1920	GB

Dansk	1901-03	DK		Fuji Cabin	1957-58	J		Kroboth	1954-55	D
Darmont	1924-39	F		Fuldamobil	1950-69	D		Kurier	1948	CS
Dasse	1894-96	B		Gaitan	1950s	E		Kurogane	1935-62	J
Daulon	1950	F		Gallati	c1982-83	USA		Kyma	1903-05	GB
David	1950-56	E		Gashopper	1980s	USA		LAD	1913-26	GB
Davis	1947-49	USA		Gasi	1921	D		La Durance	1908-10	F
DD	1949-50	VN/MA		Gasmobile	1900	USA		La Fleurantine	1906	F
De Boisse	1900-04	F		GB	1922-24	GB		Lagonda	1901-05	GB
Decolon	1957	F		Geha	1910-23	D		Lambert	1891	USA
DECSA Lisa	1982-87	RSM		Gilcolt	c1972	GB		Lamb-Kar	1950	GB
Deltamobil	1954-55	D		Girling	1913-14	GB		Lambretta		
DG Phoenix	1982-date	GB		GMT Rivelaine	1981-83	F		Rickshaw	1957-date	I/IND
Diable	1921-24	D		Gnom	1950	D		Lambro	1952	I
Diabolo	1922-27	D		Goliath	1924-33	D		Landgrebe	1921-24	D
Dickinson Morette	1903-05	GB		Gommel	1947	D		La Nef	1901-03	F
Diehlmobile	1962-64	USA		Gordon	1954-58	GB		La Torpille	1912-13	F
DMC	1913-14	GB		Gorham	1920-22	J		La Va Bon Train	1900	F
Doddsmobile	1947	CDN		Goricke	1907-08	D		Lawil A4	1984	I
Dorran	1991	USA		Gorke	1921	D		Leon Bollee	1895-98	F
D-Rad Rikscha	1951	A		Grewe & Schutte	1954-56	D		Lepoix Ding	1975	D
Dragonfly	1994-date	GB		Grice	1927	GB		Lesshaft	1925-26	D
DRK	1987-date	GB		Grinnall Scorpion	1992-date	GB		Lewis Airmobile	1937	USA
DS Malterre	1955	F		Haargaard	1950s	DK		Libelle	1952-55	A
Dual e Turconi	1899-1901	I		Harper	1921-26	GB		Lincoln	1920	GB
Dumas	1902-03	F		Heathfield				Lindsay	1900-06	GB
Dunkley	1896/1915	GB		Slingshot	1992-date	GB		Lomar Honey	1985-86	DK
Duryea	1902-06	USA		Heinkel	1956-58	D		Lomax 223/423	1983-date	GB
Duryea Gem	1916	USA		Heinkel-I	1958-61	IRL		Lomax Supa Vee	1992-date	GB
D'Yrsan	1923-28	F		Helicak	1970s	RI		Lomax Lambda 3	1993-date	GB
Eagle	1903-07	GB		Helo	1923	D		LSD	1920-24	GB
Eaglet	1948	GB		Hercules	1932-33	D		Lucciola	1948-49	I
Eastman	1899-1902	USA		Hero	1934	D		Magnet	1907-26	D
EBS	1924	D		H-M Freeway	1979-83	USA		Manocar	1952-53	F
Economic	1921-22	GB		Horrocks	1918	GB		Marocchi	1900-01	I
Edith	1953	AUS		Hostaco Bambino	1952-c57	NL		Marold	1951	A
EEC	1952-54	GB		HP	1926-28	GB		Marot-Gardon	1898-1901	F
Egan	1952	GB		HSM	1913-15	GB		Martin	1920-22	USA
Egg	1896-1900	CH		Hudson Free Spirit	1990-94	GB		Martin	1954	USA
Eibach	1924	D		Humbee-Surrey	1950-62	J		Matchless	1913-14	GB
Ekamobil	1913-14	D		Humber	1898-1905	GB		Mathis VL333	1946	F
Electra	1899-1900	D		Husqvarna	1943	S		Mayrette	1910-11	D
Electric Shopper	1964-c73	USA		Induhag	1922	D		Mazda	1931-40	J
Erla-Bond	1950-52	DK		Inter	1953-56	F		MB	1919-20	GB
Enfield Autoette	1918	GB		Internationale	1942	NL		McLachlan	1900-01	GB
Entrop	1909	NL		Isetta	1953-55	I		Meiwa	1952	J
Eric	1911-14	GB		ISSI Microbo	1953-54	I		Meister G5N	1969	A
Euricar	1930	GB		Ivry	1905-06	F/GB		Meray	1928-32	H
Europeene	1899-1903	F		Jackson	1899/1913-15	GB		Messerschmitt KR	1953-64	D
Falcon Design LX3	1983-date	GB		JBF Boxer	1992-date	GB		Metz	1909	NL
Fascination	1971	USA		Jephcott Micro	1983	GB		Meyra	1948-56	D
Favorit	1908-09	D		Jet	1955	E		Miari e Giusti	1896-99	I
Felber Autoroller	1952-54	A		JMB	1933-35	GB		Milde et Mondos	1898-1903	F
Fend Flitzer	1948-51	D		Junior	1955	E		Miles	1910-12	GB
Fend FK150	1953	D		JZR	1990-date	GB		Mini-Cat	1978-80	F
Feora	1982	USA		Kaiser	1935	D		Minima	1911	F
Ferro	1935	I		Kapi	1950-58	E		Mink	1968	GB
Fiberfab Scarab	1975-79	USA		Keinath	1949	D		Minnow	1951-52	GB
Fioretti F50	1978-81	I		Kelsey	1898	USA		Minutoli-Millo	1896	I
Fire Aero	1980s	USA		Kikos	1980-83	F		Mi-Val	1954	I
FR	1927-28	F		Klaus	1894-87	F		Mobilek	1979	GB
Framo Piccolo	1932-37	D		Knap	1898-1904	B/F		Monet-Goydon	1921-23	F
Framo Stromer	1933-37	D		Knight	1894-96	GB		Mops	1925	D
Frankl Autoroller	1949	D		Knoller	1924	D		Morford Flyer	1993-date	GB
Frisky Family 3	1959-64	GB		Knox	1900-03	USA		Morgan	1910-52	GB
Frisky Prince	1960-64	GB		Kreibich	1948-49	CS		Morin Aerocar	1948	F

Name	Years	Country		Name	Years	Country		Name	Years	Country
Morrison	1904-05	GB		Repton	1904	GB		Tibicar Bella	1979-85	I
Mosquito	c1977	GB		Revelli	1941	I		Tilli Capton	1957	AUS
Motocor	1921-24	I		Rex	1903-07	GB		Tischer	1914	USA
Motorette	1910-12	USA		Revolution	1970s	GB		Titan	1911	GB
MT	1955	E		Rheda	1898-89	F		Toboggan	1905-06	GB
Mumford Musketeer	1971-date	GB		Rieju	1955-56	E		Torpelle	1914	F
MV Bambina	1920	I		Riker	1896	USA		Tourette	1956-57	GB
Neander	1936	D		Riley	1900-07	GB		Tourist	1907-20	D
Neimann	1931	D		Rinspeed UFO	1983	CH		Tractavant	1951-52	F
New Hudson	1920	GB		ROA	1950s	E		Triad	1992-date	GB
Ninon	1930	F		Roger	1888-94	F		Tribelhorn	1918-20	CH
Nobel 200	1969-62	GB		Rogers Rascal	1980s	CDN		Tri-Car	1955	USA
NSU Max-Kabine	1954	D		Rollfix	1933-36	D		Trident	1919-20	F/GB
OD	1933	D		Romanazzi	1953	I		Triffid	1990s	GB
Omega	1925-27	GB		Roots and Venables	1896-97	GB		Trihawk	1980s	USA
Onnasch	1924	D		Rosenbauer	1950	A		Triking	1983-date	GB
Orient Express	1895-1903	D		Royal Ruby	1927	GB		Tri-Moto	1900-01	USA
OTI	1957-59	F		RW Kit Cars	1980s	GB		Trio	1993-date	GB
Pappenberger	1953	D		RWN	1928-29	D		Tripacer	1994-date	GB
Paris-Rhone	1947-50	F		SAMCA Atomo	1947-51	I		Tri-Ped	1979	USA
Pashley	1953	GB		Sanchis	1906-12	F		Tripod	1986	GB
Pelican Rickshaw	1953-57	GB		Sandford	1922-36	F		Trisport Scorpion	1990	GB
Pasquini Valentine	1976-80	I		Santler	1920s	GB		Triumph	1933	D
PB	1955	F		Sautel et Sechaud	1902-04	F		Tri-Vator	c1980	USA
Peel Manxman	1955	GBM		Schwammberger	1950	D		Trojan	1961-65	GB
Peel P50	1962-66	GBM		Scootacar	1958-65	GB		Tryker	1980s	USA
Peel Trident	1965-66	GBM		Scoot-mobile	1946	USA		Trylon	1992-date	USA
Peka	1924	D		Scott Sociable	1921-25	GB		TST	1922	GB
Pennington	1896	GB		Seal	1912-24	GB		Turner	1900-01	USA
Perfecta	1899-1903	I		Seetstu	1906-07	GB		Twike	1993-date	CH
Petit Puce	1976	F		SGS	1983	CH		Tyseley-Unicar	1911	GB
Peugeot VLV	1941-45	F		Shell Valley Apollo	1980s	USA		Utopian	1914	GB
Phanomen	1907-1927	D		Shelter	1954-58	NL		Vaghi	1920-24	I
Phoenix	1903-05	GB		Sibrava	1920-c22	CS		Velomobil	1905-07	D
Pinguin	1953-55	D		Simplex	1919-20	NL		Velorex	1954-71	CS
PMC	1912-13	GB		Sinclair C5	1985	GB		VH	1961	E
Poinard	1952	F		Singer	1900-07	GB		Villard	1925-35	F
Poirier	1928-58	F		Skip	1990-date	GB		Vimp	1955	GB
Powerdrive	1955-58	GB		Solomobil	1921-22	D		Vincent	1950s	GB
Praga	1952	CS		Souriau	1912-14	F		Vitrex Riboud	1974-80	F
Progress	1934	GB		SP Spi-Tri	1980s	USA		Addax/Gildax	1974-80	F
Publix	1947-48	USA/CDN		Speedy	1905	GB		Voiture Electroniq	1968-76	F
Pulga	1952-53	E		Stanhope	1915-22/1925	GB		Volk	1895	GB
P.Vallee Sicraf	1952-57	F		Stimson Scorcher	1976-81	GB		Wagenhals	1913-15	USA
Chantecler	1956-57	F		Stinger	1994-date	GB		Walco	1905	GB
Quadrant	1906-07	GB		Story	1941-44	NL		Wall	1911-15	GB
Quincy-Lynn				Succes	1952	B		Walmobil	1920	D
Urba Trike	1978-85	USA		Sui Tong Rickshaw	1960s-80s	RC		Walter	1908-12	A/CS
Trimuter	1980-85	USA		Sui Tong Cub	1982-83	RC		Wasp	1984	AUS
Tri-Magnum	1983-85	USA		Sunrise	1980s	USA		Weber	1899	CH
Raleigh	1933-36	GB		Sunrise Badal	1978-80	IND		Weise	1932	D
Rana Mymsa	1957	E		Super Kar	1946	USA		Wendax	1930s	D
Randall	1904	USA		Sycar	1915	GB		Wesnigk	1920-23	D
Ranger Cub	1974-76	GB		SZL	1956-69	SU		Williamson	1913-16	GB
Rapid	1899-1900	CH		Tamag	1933	D		Witkar	1970s	NL
Regina	1922-25	F		Tankette	1919-20	GB		WMC Bug	1990-date	GB
Reid	1895	USA		Tatin	1899	F		Wolseley	1896	GB
Reliant Regal	1951-62	GB		Tatra Type 49	1938	CS		XK-1	1980s	USA
Regal 3/25-3/30	1962-73	GB		TB	1919-20	GB		Xtra	1922-24	GB
Reliant Robin	1973-81	GB		Teilhol Citadine	1972-82	F		Yamata	1916	J
Reliant Rialto	1981-90/1991-date	GB		Messagette	1975-83	F		Yue Loong		
Reliant Ant	1970s-date	GB		Tempo	1933-date	D/IND		Rickshaw	1970s-date	RC
Renaux	1901-02	F		Thrift-T	1955	USA		ZAZ prototype	1954	SU
				Thurlow	1920-21	GB		Zetgelette	1923	D
								Zoe Zipper	1984	USA/J

About the Author...

Since buying his first ever car – a Bond Bug – the three-wheeler bug has always been in Chris Rees' blood. No satisfactory explanation has ever been provided by medical science. Other voyages into the strange world of three-wheelers have included the construction of a Lomax 223 for *Which Kit?* magazine in 1987 and the amputation of a Citroen 2CV to turn it into a trike. Of indeterminate age, Chris understandably lives in the vicinity of Broadmoor – just in case.

Chris Rees in France with his Lomax, circa 1989.

And About the Publisher...

Perhaps the less said, the better! Peter Filby has always preferred to think of himself as a dignified, sophisticated publishing tycoon. Then the technical staff of his magazine, *Which Kit?*, built him a Lomax and he became a changed man. He began to giggle to himself, wave at strangers, wear strange headwear and refresh the parts of his motoring brain he never previously knew were there. Such a radical new lease of life led the perpetual 'fortysomething' to become bafflingly enthusiastic about publishing this book.

And a message from both...

We'd like to have wrapped-up the definitive and exhaustively comprehensive history of three-wheelers all in one book. But the sheer volume of the things made around the world means that, for reasons of space, some have been excluded (although see our complete A to Z listing starting on page 165). As a result, there just may be, at some time in the future, a follow-up book covering 'the rest'. So we would be delighted to hear from anyone who is interested and, indeed, anyone who has further information about, and pictures of, three-wheelers. Please write to us at *Blueprint Books, 1 Howard Road, Reigate, Surrey RH2 7JE.*